Henry de Beltgens Gibbins

British Commerce and Colonies

From Elizabeth to Victoria

Henry de Beltgens Gibbins

British Commerce and Colonies
From Elizabeth to Victoria

ISBN/EAN: 9783337151508

Printed in Europe, USA, Canada, Australia, Japan

Cover: Foto ©ninafisch / pixelio.de

More available books at **www.hansebooks.com**

BRITISH COMMERCE

AND

COLONIES

FROM ELIZABETH TO VICTORIA

BY

H. DE B. GIBBINS, Litt.D., M.A.,

Author of " The Industrial History of England," " The History of Commerce in Europe," " Industry in England," etc.

THIRD EDITION

METHUEN & CO.
36 ESSEX STREET, W.C.
LONDON
1899

PREFACE

THIS review of the history of British commerce since the days of Queen Elizabeth has been written to supply the want of a short text-book, which should present the main outlines of, and facts about, our commercial progress in a simple and concise form, without going into those interesting but often elaborate details which more fitly belong to larger works. It is intended partly for those schools and colleges which now devote some attention to commercial as well as to political history, but also, it is hoped, will be of use to the general public, and especially to men of business, who take an interest in the development of our national commerce, but who have not time for a lengthened study of the subject. To some extent it supplies certain deficiencies in the author's *Industrial History of England*, as it deals with points which in that work were necessarily omitted or referred to very briefly. But it has been written quite independently of the former work.

Special attention has been paid to our colonial possessions, and to India; and it is hoped that the survey of the British Empire given at the end of the last chapter may be useful in this connection.

I have been especially fortunate in enlisting for this book the kindly help of Professor C. F. Bastable, whose authority as an economic historian and statistician is too well known to require further comment. He has not only read and corrected my work while in proof, but has also given me many most valuable suggestions and notes upon particular points, and I have to thank him very sincerely for his friendly assistance. The list of authorities at the end of the book is also extracted from his article on "British Commerce" in the *Dictionary of Political Economy*.

H. DE B. GIBBINS.

NOTTINGHAM, *May, 1893.*

PREFACE
TO THE SECOND EDITION.

———o———

THIS edition is the same as the first, except for a few corrections of misprints and other minor errors. Upon the suggestion of Professor Bastable, of Trinity College, Dublin, a table of some important dates has been added at the end of the volume. For a fuller account of industry, as distinct from commerce, students should consult the author's larger work, *Industry in England.*

H. DE B. G.

LIVERPOOL,
   October, 1896.

CONTENTS

CHAP.		PAGE
I.	INTRODUCTORY	1
II.	THE MERCHANT COMPANIES AND COMMERCIAL PROGRESS	6
III.	MONOPOLIES	15
IV.	COLONISATION	19
V.	FINANCIAL QUESTIONS OF THE SEVENTEENTH CENTURY	27
VI.	COMMERCE IN THE SEVENTEENTH CENTURY	32
VII.	COMMERCIAL INSTITUTIONS AND LEGISLATION UNDER WILLIAM III.	43
VIII.	THE METHUEN TREATY AND THE UNION WITH SCOTLAND	52
IX.	THE TREATY OF UTRECHT AND THE SOUTH SEA BUBBLE	58
X.	THE CONQUEST OF INDIA, A.D. 1600-1761	65
XI.	THE CONQUEST OF INDIA, A.D. 1761-1857	73
XII.	THE AMERICAN COLONIES AND THEIR SEPARATION	81

CONTENTS.

XIII. THE INDUSTRIAL REVOLUTION AND THE CONTINENTAL WAR 88
XIV. ENGLAND DURING THE WAR, AND THE UNION WITH IRELAND 94
XV. COMMERCE SINCE 1815 — THE ERA OF FREE TRADE 102
XVI. RECENT CHANGES IN OUR TRADE AND EASTERN AFFAIRS 113
XVII. MODERN COLONIAL DEVELOPMENT . . 118
APPENDIX I. THE BRITISH EMPIRE; A LIST OF OUR POSSESSIONS AND COLONIES, WITH THEIR COMMERCIAL PRODUCTS 127
APPENDIX II. NOTE ON AUTHORITIES . . . 134
A TABLE OF IMPORTANT DATES 135
INDEX 137

BRITISH COMMERCE.

CHAPTER I

INTRODUCTORY.

§ 1. **English Supremacy of Recent Growth.** — It has often been remarked, though the remark is frequently not fully realised, that the supremacy of Great Britain in matters of industry and commerce is a supremacy of very recent growth. As a matter of fact our position has been won in little more than two centuries, and chiefly in the 17th and 18th. "In the 14th century the whole of the external and much of the internal trade of the country had been in the hands of foreigners; in the 15th our merchants began to push their way from point to point in the Mediterranean and the Baltic; in the 16th they followed slowly in the wake of other adventurers,[1] or tried to establish themselves in unkindly regions which had attracted no one else.[2] When Elizabeth ascended the throne, England appears to

[1] *e.g.* The English followed the Spaniards in N. and S. America and West Indies, and the Portuguese and Dutch in the East.
[2] *e.g.* The shores of N. America, where at first Gilbert and Raleigh failed to plant a colony.

have been behind other nations of Western Europe in the very industrial arts and commercial enterprise on which her present reputation is chiefly based."[1]

§ 2. **The Mercantile System.**—But in the days of Queen Elizabeth a new and vigorous departure was made, and a scheme of commercial policy was inaugurated which, though not new, was now carried out in a more systematic manner than at any previous time. The policy was that of the "Mercantile System." Its main object was the attainment of national wealth and power; and the means to that end were (1) the obtaining of wealth in the form of bullion; (2) the possession of a large amount of shipping generally and of a good navy in particular; (3) the promotion of agriculture and manufactures at home. To gain these ends we find that (1) the export of bullion was, as far as possible, checked, if not actually forbidden, and attempts were made to procure a favourable "balance of trade" for England in all her dealings with other countries; (2) the English shipping industry was encouraged by a series of Navigation Acts, from those of Elizabeth (5 Eliz. c. 5) to the more famous Acts of 1651 and 1660, while careful attention was also paid to the fisheries (5 Eliz. c. 5) and to the supply of naval stores, with an ultimate view to the welfare of shipping; (3) agriculture was protected by Corn Laws, forbidding the import of foreign corn, but allowing and even encouraging by bounties its export, so that plenty of corn might be grown at home; while similar measures are also taken for the encouragement of home manufactures. For example, imports of foreign manufactures were forbidden by 5 Eliz. c. 7, and Elizabeth insisted that all her subjects should wear English made caps (13 Eliz. c. 19).

[1] Cunningham, *Growth of English Industry and Commerce*, ii. 2.

INTRODUCTORY. 3

§ 3. **Criticisms of that Policy.**—Such is a brief outline of the main points of the policy of the Mercantile System. The policy has often been severely criticised, and is now generally admitted to be wrong, or at least unsuitable for the present circumstances of our commerce. But there is no doubt that, while it prevailed, British commerce and industry throve and flourished, and our power as a nation increased. Perhaps commerce would have flourished even more without these regulations, but it is doubtful if our political power would have been so great. At any rate we see from the 16th to the 19th century an era of wonderful progress. "England first outstripped Holland, and then raised an empire in East and West, on the ruins of French dependencies."[1] Agriculture was improved and manufacturing industries were developed at home, while new possessions were taken and new colonies settled abroad.

§ 4. **England and Spain.**—But in the time of Elizabeth all these things were not yet accomplished. In those days the most powerful country in Europe was Spain, and the power of Spain seemed to block the way to English enterprise. Hence, unfortunately perhaps, but still unavoidably, England was bound to come into conflict with Spain so soon as ever English merchants tried to extend our foreign commerce. Spain had then the monopoly of the riches of the East and West, and if England was to break through that monopoly, a fight with the Spaniards was inevitable. This alone was a sufficient cause of hostility between the two countries; but, added to this, there was the irreconcilable difference of religion, which served to make matters worse. Spain was Roman Catholic ; England was Protest-

[1] Cunningham, ii. 17, which see for a clear account of the Mercantile System.

ant, and when, in 1579, Elizabeth entered into an offensive and defensive alliance with the Protestant States of Holland, who were throwing off the yoke of Spain, she practically declared war against the Spanish king. From this time forward both the English and the Dutch strove by all means in their power to break the Spanish monopoly both in the East and West, and finally succeeded, though before they had done so the two Protestant nations began to quarrel with each other.

§ 5. **Some Elizabethan Sea Captains.**—Now, just two years before Queen Elizabeth took the side of the Dutch States, Sir Francis Drake set out on his famous voyage round the world, with the object of damaging as far as possible the power of Spain in her colonies. He set sail, with Elizabeth's sanction, in 1577, and plundered all the Spanish towns on the coasts of Chili and Peru, seizing immense booty therefrom. Then crossing the Pacific Ocean he came back round the Cape of Good Hope, and on returning to England in 1580, was knighted by the Queen for his achievements. Another great navigator was Sir Martin Frobisher, who set sail in 1576, in order to try and discover a North-West passage to India. After failing in that, he accompanied Drake in a voyage to the West Indies (1584). John Davis, again, who died in 1605, was another explorer who made three voyages in search of a North-West passage to the pacific, and then in 1591 went sailing about the South Seas with Thomas Cavendish, a celebrated navigator, who was the second Englishman to sail round the globe, but who died upon his voyage (1592) with Davis. Another very enterprising seaman was Sir John Hawkins (born 1520, died 1595) who passed most of his early days in making voyages in the interests of foreign commerce, and, as all

INTRODUCTORY. 5

know, was the first Englishman to begin trading in negroes (1562). He was the companion of Frobisher in the expedition to the Spanish Main in 1590, and of Sir Francis Drake in another to the West Indies, but on this last voyage he died. Then, finally, we must not forget the unfortunate Sir Walter Raleigh (born 1552, died 1618) who began his naval career by a voyage to Newfoundland, sent several colonising expeditions to America,[1] twice sailed to Guiana to search for El Dorado, the land of gold, and was at last basely beheaded by James I. It is to these great sailors and sea captains that we owe very largely the growth of our British commerce, for by their daring deeds and discoveries[2] they opened out new fields of enterprise to our merchants, who in course of time followed up the paths of commerce thus indicated by forming various "companies" for trading in foreign parts. One of the greatest of these associations, the East India Company, was fortunate enough to secure the personal services of John Davis. Of this company and others we will now speak.

[1] See p. 20.
[2] The attempts to find a North-West passage to India were due to the fact that the Spaniards and Portuguese tried to monopolise the sea-route round the Cape and held the Eastern trade almost entirely in their own hands. Hence it was necessary to find some other route in order to avoid conflicts with these two powers. Cf. the Levant Company's attempt to find an overland route to India, § 7.

CHAPTER II.

THE MERCHANT COMPANIES AND COMMERCIAL PROGRESS.

§ 6. **The Levant Company.**—We must now devote a few words to a consideration of these Merchant Companies that form so prominent a feature in the history of the 16th and 17th centuries.

Although the East India Company which we have just mentioned became in later years the greatest of all, it was by no means as important as some of the others when it was first founded. Indeed it owes its origin largely to another company, very celebrated in its day, the Levant, or Turkey Company, which was chartered in 1581, although trade with the Levant had been going on for thirty years before this. In the year 1581 a number of prominent merchants were incorporated into a company for trading to Turkey, to which country their charter declared they had, " at their own great cost and charges, found out and opened a trade not heretofore, in the memory of any man living, known to be commonly used and frequented by way of merchandise." After trading for some years, they were reconstituted in 1605, under a new charter of James I., as " The Merchants of England Trading to the Levant Seas," and continued to exist as a company till well into the present century. They had an English envoy, or representative, to reside within the dominions of the Sultan of

Turkey, with authority to appoint consuls in the various Eastern towns to superintend our trade. This trade for some time was very flourishing, our exports being chiefly woollen manufactures, watches, and tin, while the company imported to England in return, large amounts of silk, cotton, mohair, drugs, currants, jewels, and other well-known products of Asia Minor, Turkey, and Greece. In Mun's *Discourse of Trade from England to East India*, a treatise published [1] in 1621, it is asserted that of all Europe, England then drove the most profitable trade to Turkey by reason of the vast quantities of broadcloth, tin, and other goods which were exported thither. Other writers of the 17th century independently confirm this statement.

§ 7. **Attempts to reach India.**—Ever since its foundation, this company had manifested a strong desire to open up direct commercial intercourse with India and the East Indies. The Portuguese had the Eastern trade by sea at that time almost completely in their hands; and as they were supported by Spain it was necessary for the Levant Company to find an overland route, if they wished to escape a conflict. They made various attempts, only partially successful, to do this; but at length gave it up; and meanwhile the East India Company was formed. The proposal to form it was made at a meeting of about a hundred of the chief merchants of London on September 22nd, 1599, at which many members of the Levant Company were present. A capital of £30,000 was subscribed, and at length, on the last day of the year 1600, Queen Elizabeth gave the charter to the body called " The Governor and Company of the Merchants of London Trading into the East Indies," that was many years afterwards to win for us our present Indian Empire.

[1] Or, perhaps, as McCulloch thinks, in 1609.

§ 8. Early Days of the East India Company.—The

first governor of this company, Alderman Thomas Smith, was also one of the leading members of the Levant Company. No time was lost by the new company in fitting out a small fleet to engage in the East Indian trade, and in April, 1601, Captain Lancaster, who had been raised to the rank of an admiral, set out for the East with five small ships laden chiefly with bullion, iron, tin, broadcloth, cutlery, and glass. He returned home in September, 1603, after a tedious voyage, with the two largest of his ships laden with pepper, and two others with cargoes of spices, calicoes, and other Indian manufactures and products. But as yet fortune did not seem to favour the ventures of the new company; and many vessels were lost at sea, though in 1609 an expedition under Captain Middleton brought back such a valuable cargo of nutmegs and mace as to produce a dividend of 211 per cent. In the same year a new charter was obtained by the company by which their privilege of exclusive trade (which was originally granted for fifteen years) was made perpetual, though with a reservation that the Government should be allowed to dissolve it at any time with three years' notice. After this the affairs of the company became more prosperous, as the following table of the percentage of profits made will readily show [1]:—

Voyage of 1610 to 1613	121 per cent.
Voyage of 1611 to 1615	218 ,,
The 9th voyage	160 ,,
The 10th voyage	148 ,,
The 11th voyage	340 ,,
The 12th voyage	134 ,,

[1] Craik, *Hist. Brit. Com.*, vol. ii., p. 15.

Against these apparently high profits there must be reckoned serious losses of ships wrecked at sea, or captured by the Dutch, who at that time were our bitter rivals in the East. Up to 1620, for instance, the company had sent 79 ships to India, of which 34 returned home richly laden, 8 were lost at sea, 12 were captured, and 4 were worn out; the total exports to India since the formation of the company had been £840,376, while the imports from India cost £356,288, and had been sold in England for the sum of £1,914,600. From this sum, however, must be deducted an item of £84,008, which represents the cost of fights with the Dutch.[1] Indeed the hostility of the Dutch was for a long time a most formidable obstacle to the success of the company, as this enterprising nation in their endeavours to obtain an exclusive monopoly of the spice trade did not scruple to adopt any and every means to obtain their objects. Hence quarrels and disputes, often of a violent character, arose between them and the English, the most serious of which resulted in a massacre by the Dutch of all the English traders and settlers in the Island of Amboyna, in 1622.

§ 9. **Other Companies.**—We must, however, now leave the history of the East India Company for the present, in order to mention at least the names of other associations of some celebrity at this epoch. In referring to these trading companies, we may anticipate chronological order a little, and quote the evidence of Lewis Roberts, who published a work called *The Merchant's Map of Commerce*, at London, in 1638, wherein he mentions a large number of trading associations. We find, of

[1] Mun's *Discourse of Trade from England to the East Indies*, p. 10, first edition, or p. 31 in McCulloch's reprint.

course, the Levant Company still enjoying considerable prosperity; then he mentions the East India Company, whose affairs, however, in James I.'s reign, were in a somewhat depressed condition; and then comes the Ancient Company of Merchant Adventurers, who traded with Hamburg, Rotterdam, and other cities of the Netherlands. Next we have the Eastland and Muscovy (or Russian) Companies trading with Russia; the French Company trading with France; and besides these companies, Roberts mentions also other merchants, apparently not incorporated, who traded with Spain, Portugal, and with various Italian cities.[1]

From this list supplied by Roberts, it will be seen that our commerce was by this time fairly extensive, and besides the countries alluded to just above, he mentions, though as of secondary value, various colonial possessions that were now slowly rising into importance. "The famous Barbary trade had indeed sunk into insignificance, and the trade with Guinea and Benin, off the West Coast of Africa, was (he says) of a petty character." But that our home and colonial trade was of growing importance may be seen from the closing sentence of his remarks: "Neither need I nominate the home-land commerce of this country to Scotland and Ireland; neither go about to particularise the large traffic of this island to their late plantations of Newfoundland, Somers Islands (*i.e.*, the Bermudas), Virginia, Barbadoes, and New England and other places which rightly challenge an interest in the present trade and traffic of this kingdom." From all that has been said above, it will be seen that our foreign commerce in the 17th century was rapidly attaining considerable proportions.

[1] See note at end of this chapter on joint-stock and regulated companies.

§ 10. **Commerce since the 16th Century.**—In quoting Roberts we have indeed gone beyond the reign of Elizabeth; but we may safely say that his statements represent very fairly the state of things at the close of her reign. It has been well remarked that in the course of the long reign of this Queen the commerce and navigation of England had risen through the whole of the space that in the life of a human being would be described as intervening between the close of infancy and the commencement of manhood. " It was the age of the vigorous boyhood and adolescence of the national industry, when although its ultimate conquests were still afar off, the path that led to them was fairly entered upon, and every step was one of progress and buoyant with hope." We shall understand the truth of this remark better perhaps if we glance back for a moment at the state of English commerce in the first half of the 16th century, when the movement of trade as estimated by Schanz in the reign of Henry VIII. was as follows :—*Imports:* 10,060 tuns of wine, 3028 cwt. of wax, making with other imports a total real value of £402,092, but officially estimated at £284,360. *Exports:* 98,132 pieces of cloth, 5785 sacks of wool, 14,056 hides, 4387 pieces of worsted, 8931 cwt. of tin, with other exports giving a total estimated value of £427,830, officially stated at £293,287.[1]

§ 11. **Causes of Growth of English Commerce.**— From these figures we perceive the great growth of the woollen industry in England, and observe that our country now exports far more manufactured woollen cloth than it used to do in the Middle Ages. In former times the English had not been able to manufacture the wool which they grew so largely, but when we had learnt from foreigners

[1] *Dict. Pol. Econ.*, art. "British Commerce," p. 343.

the art of manufacturing both woollen and worsted goods, we began to make our competition felt even amongst the Flemish, who had formerly been our rivals and indeed our superiors. Moreover, the development of our export trade was aided to some extent by the great change of money values in the 16th century, when, it will be remembered, the Spaniards discovered the gold and silver mines of South America and poured so large a quantity of the precious metals into the European markets. For a thousand years before this there had been no large addition to the amount of metallic money in circulation, and indeed the stock had been at certain times if anything somewhat reduced. The rapid rise in prices which followed upon the flow of gold and silver into the commercial centres of Europe from the gold mines of Mexico and Peru stimulated the already growing import of English products into the Netherlands, for the rise of prices only made itself felt some years later in England (1570) than it did on the Continent.

§ 12. **The Flemish and the Hansa.**—Moreover, apart from the stimulus thus caused by the rise in prices, which after all could not be a stimulus of a lasting nature, the political events which took place in the Netherlands at the close of the 16th century contributed to give further and more favourable opportunities to English merchants. Everyone knows that the Netherlands at this time were the most flourishing centres of industry, manufacture, and commerce in Northern Europe, and that they were politically under the dominion of the Roman Catholic empire of Spain, against whose power they finally revolted. They had to suffer terrible persecutions, and their country was invaded by Spanish armies. In 1585 Antwerp was captured and sacked by the Spaniards, so that most of its trade passed over to Amsterdam and London; and from this time forward London instead of Antwerp became the largest commercial centre of North-Western Europe. At the same time large numbers of Flemish weavers came over to England and settled in the Eastern counties, bringing with them both skill and capital, which helped to increase our manufacturing trade and to develop our exports.[1]

Throughout Elizabeth's reign, in fact, there was a continual migration of Protestant refugees to our shores; and Elizabeth and our statesmen had the sagacity to encourage these industrious and wealthy emigrants. Her foresight was well rewarded, for it was noted that in 1588 there were 38 Flemish merchants established in London who subscribed £5,000 towards the defence of their adopted country against the Spanish Armada. Thus the great Reformation conflict between Roman Catholic and Protestant in Europe resulted in this case also in additional commercial greatness to England. Finally we may mention as significant of the growing power of our own merchants, that the London factory of the Hansa League, which for centuries had monopolised the trade between this country and the North Sea and Baltic ports, was closed in 1598 after one or two previous attempts had been made to abolish it. Thus was removed the last trace of a time when the commerce of England was conducted by foreigners and the new era of commercial and maritime progress begins.

§ 13. **Restoration of the Currency. The Royal Exchange.**—At home two events of considerable commercial importance took place in Elizabeth's reign: the restoration of the currency and the foundation of the Royal Exchange.

[1] Compare my *Industrial History*, p. 96, and the chapter on "Manufacturing Districts of Europe," in my *Commerce in Europe*, p. 83 *sqq*.

For some time past the currency had been in a very deteriorated condition, owing to its debasement by Henry VIII., by Somerset under Edward VI. (1551), and also by Mary, and this was, of course, a great disadvantage both to home and foreign trade. Elizabeth therefore in 1559 made arrangements for gradually calling in this base money, and by 1561 it was all withdrawn from circulation and a fresh coinage issued. The Royal Exchange owes its origin to the famous merchant, Sir Thomas Gresham (born 1519, died 1579), and was finished in 1570. Before that time the merchants of London used to meet in the open air in Lombard Street for the transaction of much of their business, but this inconvenience was now avoided.

Note on Joint-stock and Regulated Companies.—The companies mentioned in the preceding chapter were divided into two classes: (1) *regulated* companies, "into which any English subject could obtain admission on understood terms, and the various members of which traded, each with his own capital, but according to the regulations of the company." Such were the Levant and Eastland Companies. "But there were also other societies of merchants which traded on a joint stock; each member subscribed as much to the common fund and obtained a share in any profits that were made." Such were the Royal African and East India Companies. See Cunningham, ii. 124.

CHAPTER III.

MONOPOLIES.

§ 14. **The Monopoly System.**—The 17th century, the early years of which are marked by the accession of James I. in 1603, saw the policy of the Mercantile System still actively pursued. It also saw the progress of the system of monopoly, which was one of the methods by which both politicians and merchants at that time sought to promote our trade. The possession of a monopoly means the possession of the *sole right* to deal in a certain article or to trade with a certain country; and this sole right might be granted either to individuals or to companies,[1] or indeed might be claimed by a nation, as, *e.g.*, when England claimed the sole right to trade with her American colonies, and tried to force them to deal only with her, and forbade them to carry on manufactures on their own account.

§ 15. **Monopolies and the Crown.**—At the close of the 16th century it had become quite a regular practice to grant monopolies for the exclusive sale or manufacture of particular articles, and the number of these had so increased that Parliament[2] had complained of them severely during the latter part of Queen Elizabeth's reign. Elizabeth had yielded to the representations of her Parliament; but

[1] *e.g.* Sir John Packington had the monopoly of the manufacture of starch (1595); the East India Company had the sole right to trade with India.

[2] It is interesting here to notice that this parliamentary struggle about

James I. used his prerogative to create so many new monopolies that public expostulation became stronger than ever, until at last (in 1609) he thought it well to proclaim a general suspension of them. Nevertheless, after 1614, during the period when James ruled without a Parliament, the number of monopolies again increased; until at length, when Parliament was called together once more in 1621, their suppression was one of the main points mentioned amongst the grievances which the House of Commons tried to redress. Three patents were chiefly complained of: (1) those on inns and hostelries, by which one man was allowed to licence all the inns in a town and therefore endeavoured to set up as many as possible; (2) the monopoly of alehouses; and (3) that of gold and silver thread. The first and third of these were possessed by Sir Giles Mompesson, who gained great wealth thereby. Most of the monopolies, however, were abolished by the Act 21, Jac. I., cap. 3 (1624), though some few were specially retained as being for the public advantage.

§ 16. **Fisheries, Shipping, and the Cloth Trade.**—The complaint against monopolies was only one amongst the many other complaints of the decay of national trade and industry made at this time, but in spite of these outcries the country was still continuing on the whole to advance steadily in wealth and prosperity.[1] Among the new fields

monopolies shows already the beginnings of the great fight between the Parliament and the Crown that came to a climax under Charles I. The Parliament was trying to regain rights which had for a long time been in abeyance, and the Crown to retain prerogatives which it had hitherto exercised unchecked. Monopolies were often used by the sovereign as forming a convenient method of raising money, paying ministers, or rewarding favourites.

[1] Cf the statistics at the end of this chapter.

of enterprise which were opened out to our merchants and sailors was that of the Northern Fisheries, into which the Russian Company entered (of course with a monopoly) in 1613, and carried on the whale fishery which had been begun some time previously by private adventurers. At the same time our shipping was greatly increasing in numbers. It is stated by Sir William Monson [1] that at James I.'s accession there were no more than 400 ships in England of 400 tons burden, whereas twelve years later the author of a pamphlet called "The Trade's Increase" (1615), gives an account of English shipping which shows that its numbers had very considerably increased during the few years before which he wrote. He mentions specially the Newcastle coal trade as employing in itself 400 vessels, while Malynes mentions that there were 250 more employed in the Newfoundland fisheries. Of our home industries, the woollen trade was now established as the leading manufacture, and was increasing its export. Indeed, the trade in wool and woollen cloths was still the great staple trade of the kingdom. We find, however, that even at this time the imperfect manner in which the cloth was dressed and dyed by English manufacturers was very prejudicial to the increase of trade, and Sir Walter Raleigh, among others, called the attention of James I. to this point. At first James tried to cure the evil by absolutely prohibiting any undyed cloths to be exported (1608), and at the same time granted to one Alderman Cockayne a patent giving him the exclusive right of the dyeing and dressing of woollen cloths. Flemish and German dyers, however, promptly replied to this measure by prohibiting the importation of all English dyed cloths; whereby the wool trade was thrown into such confusion

[1] *Naval Tracts*, quoted in Craik, ii. 31.

that it was found necessary to abolish Cockayne's patent and to remove other restrictions which had been laid upon the trade. On the other hand, a Dutch dyer was invited to come and settle in England in order to teach our manufacturers his art, and as time went on they improved both in this and other branches of the industry.

The general growth of our trade throughout the 17th century may be seen clearly from the following table (from the *Dict. of Pol. Econ.*, p. 344), with which we conclude this chapter.

Year.	Imports.	Exports.	Total.
1613	2,141,151	2,487,435	4,628,586
1622	2,619,315	2,320,436	4,939,751
1662	4,016,019	2,022,812	6,038,831
1669	4,196,139	2,063,274	6,259,413
1699	5,640,506	6,788,166	12,428,672

CHAPTER IV

COLONISATION.[1]

§ 17. **First Attempts at Colonisation.**—Besides the two main features (of commercial enterprise conducted by large companies and the Monopoly System) which we have just mentioned above, there remain two other features of great importance to be noticed in the 17th century generally, and in the reign of James I. in particular. These are the development of colonisation and the various rearrangements of national finance. We will take the question of colonisation first. In the 17th century, when the power of Spain was beginning to decay, we find English, Dutch, French, and Danes all endeavouring to found colonial empires of one kind or another, both in the East and West. But South and Central America were left practically untouched, because the power of Spain was still too strong in those regions to be interfered with. We have not space here to go into the reasons which dictated the colonial policy of other nations, but it should be noticed that as regards English colonisation two great factors are prominent—commercial

[1] Cf. Caldecott's *English Colonisation and Empire*, pp. 1-43, and Payne's *European Colonies*, pp. 15-32.

enterprise and religion. The first commercial stimulus came from the system of trading by companies, and the religious influence arose from the dissensions between various religious sects and the Church of England. Our colonies may be said to date from the time of the great navigators of Queen Elizabeth's reign, whom we have already mentioned, though, as is well known, the North American Continent was discovered nearly 100 years before their time by John Cabot (1497). The first attempts at colonisation were made by the Spaniards (in 1521 and afterwards) on the coast of Florida, and they were followed by the French in 1562. It was the French also who, soon after 1575, began to make settlements in the North of America, that is in Canada, Cape Breton, and Nova Scotia, which was then called Acadia. Nova Scotia was seized by England in the war of Spanish Succession (1713), and Canada in the Seven Years' War of 1757 to 1763. But the first attempt at colonisation proper was made in 1578 by Frobisher, who was followed by Sir Humphrey Gilbert (1579 to 1583), who twice failed to plant a settlement. He again was followed by Sir Walter Raleigh, who also made two attempts, the first of which was for some time successful and was begun in what is now North Carolina. Finally, early in King James's reign (1607), the London Company despatched an expedition to which must be given the honour of the first permanent settlement of the English in North America. This settlement took place on the banks of the James river in Virginia.

§ 18. **Colonisation by Companies.**—The mention of this London company recalls to us the fact that in the first half of the 17th century a large number of companies for colonisation were incorporated, most of whom looked to America for the realisation of their projects. There were the Virginia Company, the Bermuda Company, the Newfoundland Company, the New England Company, the Providence Company, the Canada Company, the Massachusetts Bay Company, and the Nova Scotia Company. And besides these American associations there were the First African Company (which was re-constituted four times) and the Guiana Company, which last never did anything. There were also several charters granted after 1650, though most of these were re-constitutions of old companies on a new basis, as was the case in the New Royal African Company. In Charles II.'s reign there were many such new charters. The first charter of the Hudson's Bay Company, granted in 1670, should be specially noticed.

Such was one method of promoting colonisation in the 17th century, but sometimes charters were granted not to companies but to single individuals. Thus the British Carribbee Islands were so granted to a single "lord" in 1627; Maryland (1629) was granted to Lord Baltimore; the Bahamas and Carolina in 1670. Now, in all the charters granted, whether to companies or to lord proprietors, we see the same spirit of monopoly that is visible in every other department of commercial enterprise at this time. Nearly all the grants are couched in the same terms. Their *raison d'être* was the monopoly of trade, and "the sole privilege to pass and to trade" to certain places is the main provision in all of them. Most of them were regulated by a Governor and a Court of Directors, who could make laws and imprison malefactors, but they were, of course, subject more or less to the Crown, though the supervision by the supreme government was of a very vague character. It was part of the policy of the companies to induce settlers to go to their foreign possessions, and to keep these settlers under a kind of control; but this system led to great confusion, because the government of the company, although trying to attract free settlers, nevertheless regulated everything according to their own profit, and practically denied the right of settlers to enjoy the fruits of their industry. Hence we find frequent complaints by settlers against the monopoly of the company which deprived them of their profits, and this condition of affairs was, in later years, severely commented upon by the great economist, Adam Smith.[1] Indeed, government was not so much the object of these institutions as the keeping up of their monopoly and the gaining of large profits.

§ 19. **Colonisation by Settlers.**—In spite of, or perhaps because of the arrangements for colonisation made by the companies we have just mentioned, there was not a very large influx of settlers to our American colonies until the reigns of James I. and Charles I., when the religious differences between the Puritans and the Church of England caused many of the former to seek a refuge in a land, which, though it was far off, was yet not entirely a foreign country, but which afforded them a free scope for the exercise of their religious opinions, and where they could become independent of any established church—so independent, in fact, that from being persecuted themselves, they took to persecuting others with much severity. It was to the New England group of settlements that this migration of the Puritans was chiefly directed. The Non-Conformists known as the Pilgrim Fathers sailed from England in the "Mayflower" in 1620, and after landing in

---

[1] *Wealth of Nations*, Bk. iv., ch. 7, and especially p. 155, vol. ii. (Clarendon Press edition.)

COLONISATION.

Plymouth Bay, made a permanent occupation of the country round about. Their relations with the natives were on the whole friendly, and they continued to make fresh settlements, namely New Hampshire (1622), Massachusetts (1628), Rhode Island (1631), and Connecticut (1633), though this last settlement involved the New Englanders in two Indian wars. This group of northern colonies became, on the whole, the most powerful of all the 13 settlements that were made on the eastern coast of America before the War of Independence. They formed themselves in 1643 into a federation known as "The United Colonies of New England" which in later times formed the germ of what is now the United States.

Colony.	Date of Foundation.	How Founded.
I. Virginia Group—		
Virginia	1606	By the London Company
Maryland	1632	Charter given to Lord Baltimore
N. and S. Carolina	1663	Proprietors
Georgia	1733	By General Oglethorpe
II. New York Group—		
New York	1664	⎫
New Jersey	1664	⎬ Taken from the Dutch
Delaware	1664	⎭
Pennsylvania	1682	Purchased by William Penn from Charles II.
III. New England Group—		
New Hampshire	1622	⎫
Massachusetts	1628	⎬ Colonised by Puritan Settlers
Rhode Island	1631	⎬
Connecticut	1633	⎭

Such, then, was the two-fold origin, commercial and religious, of our North American colonies, and the influence of this origin may perhaps be seen in the fact that the present inhabitants of the United States are essentially a commercially minded and Protestant people. We conclude this hasty sketch of the rise of our American colonies with a short table (see page 23) showing the order in which they were founded.

§ 20. **Various Classes of Colonies.**—Besides these American colonies, England founded several others in the West Indies and in other parts of the world, but none of these (except those founded in this century in Australia) were of the same type as the New England settlements, because they were not populated by large numbers of genuine English settlers. Taking all the colonies together, we may divide them into four kinds : firstly, the factories ; secondly, provinces ; thirdly, plantations ; and fourthly, colonies proper. The *factory* was simply a trading station where a few agents or merchants lived in order to trade with the natives, but where no regular colony settlement was made. The colonies of the Portuguese and the Dutch were often of this description, and our first settlements in India, such as Surat and Bombay, were the same ; while at the present time our stations on the West Coast of Africa are merely factories. The greatest example of a *province* in the history of the modern world is undoubtedly our present empire of India, for here the native inhabitants already in possession of the land are governed by a superior power that develops and administrates the resources of the country. In the early history of colonies, we find the Spanish colonies of Mexico and Peru generally took this form of the province ; but as the Spaniards tried to do as little as possible for the people, and get as much as possible out of them, their rule became, in the long run, a complete failure. The *plantation* was a totally different kind of settlement, its chief object being the employment of the capital of those who settled upon the land, while the necessary labour was performed by the original natives. Native labour was often reduced to subjection, if not to slavery, as was the case in the West Indies, and to some extent in Virginia and other of our North American settlements. The Plantation System was rendered necessary by the circumstances of the climate in these hot regions, which were not quite suitable for English labour, and made it necessary, therefore, either to use the native labour already existing, or else to import labour from abroad, as was done till the present century by introducing slaves, and, after the abolition of slavery, by making use of coolies. Jamaica may be regarded as a typical English plantation colony.[1] The *colony proper*, the last and greatest of these four methods of colonisation, is formed by the emigration of large bodies of capable and energetic settlers from the home country to another land, which they occupy, develop, and govern for themselves. Our former North American colonies, and our present Australian colonies, are well-known examples of this. We here add a list of English colonies founded in the 17th century (see next page), but for a complete list of all our possessions must refer the reader to the appendix.

[1] Cf. the chapter on "The Plantations" in Payne's *European Colonies*, p. 65 *sqq.*; and for the four types of colonies, the article on "Colonies" in the *Dict. of Pol. Econ.*

Name of Colony.	How Founded.
India	By East India Company
Barbadoes	Patent granted to Lord Carlisle
St. Christopher.	Colonised by Settlers
Nevis	Do. do.
Montserrat	Do. do.
Jamaica	Taken from Spaniards by free Settlers, and Plantation
Antigua	By Settlers
Anguilla	Do.
Virgin Islands	By English Planters
Bahamas	Granted to Sir. Robt. Heath
Bermudas	Settled by Somers and others
Gold Coast	By a Company

CHAPTER V.

FINANCIAL QUESTIONS OF THE 17TH CENTURY.

§ 21. **Bate's Case and the Book of Rates.**—It is now time to consider some of the financial difficulties arising in the 17th century which led, among many other causes, to the great struggle between King and Parliament which is sometimes called by the title of "The Struggle against Absolute Monarchy." The beginning of the strife is seen very early in James I.'s reign in what is now known to history as Bate's case, or the case of Impositions. The facts of this case are as follows :—Tunnage and poundage, which had been granted *for life* to every king since Henry V., included a duty of 2s. 6d. per cwt. on currants. James, by his own authority, imposed another 5s., and thus trebled the duty.[1] John Bate, a merchant of the Levant Company, refused to pay this (1606) on the ground that the tax could only be imposed lawfully by Parliament. The case being brought before the Court of Exchequer, judgment was given for the Crown. In this judgment it was laid down that the Royal power was double : (1) it was *ordinary* or unchangeable, without authority of Parliament, and (2) *absolute*, varying according to the King's wisdom. Moreover, under this "absolute" power came all matters of commerce,

[1] Cf. *Dict. Pol. Econ.*, p. 125, and also Hall's *History of the Customs Revenue*, vol. i., ch. iv.

including customs duties. This decision was naturally very pleasing to James, since with the growing increase of commerce in his reign it promised to make the customs revenue considerably larger than it had been before. Relying, therefore, on this decision, Cecil, Earl of Salisbury, then Lord Treasurer, published in 1608 a Book of Rates imposing fresh duties upon many articles, by which the Crown obtained an additional £70,000 of revenue per annum. But in 1610 the Commons declared that such impositions without the consent of Parliament were unconstitutional, and petitioned (as they did several times afterwards) for their removal. From this time forward the question constantly came up in the struggle between Parliament and the Crown. It came up, for instance, in the well-known case of tunnage and poundage.

§ 22. **Tunnage and Poundage.**—Like the question of monopolies, the other financial questions which now arose were concerned very closely with the Royal prerogative, and perhaps the most important, and at any rate the most familiar, of these questions was that of tunnage and poundage, that arose in the first year of Charles I.'s reign. This tax was a duty, which, after some fluctuations, was eventually fixed at 3s. upon every tun of wine and 5s. per cent. on all goods imported, and was, as far as we know, first voted by the House of Commons as far back as 1308. The original motive of the duty was that it should be applied to the protection of the merchant navy, but it soon began to be looked upon as a regular part of the Royal revenue, and therefore, when, in 1625, the House of Commons, on Charles I.'s accession, proceeded to vote it to the King, not for life, but only for one year, a great deal of excitement was naturally aroused. The House of Lords, siding with the

King, rejected the bill from the House of Commons, which had granted the payment for only one year; but when Charles tried to levy the tax by his own Royal authority, the London merchants refused to pay it. Finally, after much conflict, Charles was compelled, in 1630, to consent to an Act renouncing the power of levying this tax without the consent of Parliament, and in 1641 the prerogative of levying customs on merchandise was abolished by an Act which granted tunnage and poundage for two months only. It was again granted for life to Charles II. and James II., but for short periods only to William III. It was applied in the reign of Anne to the diminishing of the National Debt, and was finally abolished by Pitt's Consolidation Act, 1787.[1]

§ 23. **Expedients of Charles I. to Raise a Revenue.** —But tunnage and poundage was only one of the many expedients to which Charles I. found himself compelled to resort in order to provide for his expenditure. As trade increased in the days of peace the resistance to this particular tax died away, and the King proceeded to try further means to increase his revenue. He laid heavy fines upon all those who, while possessing the due qualifications, had refrained from taking knighthood at his coronation. He again revived the grant of monopolies for the sale of special articles, among which the monopolies for selling soap, starch, and beer (1634) were very strongly resented. The number of fines was increased by the system of creating new offences by proclamation, and then fining people for infringing the proclamation. The Star Chamber also exacted large sums, and a survey of the forests was made, after which all lands which had been taken by landowners from the borders of the forests were now

[1] *Dict. Eng. Hist.* s.v.

resumed and became the possession of the Crown, while those owners who had thus encroached upon the forest land were heavily fined. The system of forced loans, otherwise known as benevolences, had been used before by James I.; and though Charles did not revive this practice, his methods of taxation were so unparliamentary and, according to the advancing views of that time, so unconstitutional, that in 1628 the famous Petition of Rights was presented, which, amongst other things, claimed that no freeman should be required to give any gift, loan, or tax without the consent of Parliament. This claim was assented to by the King. It was not long after this, however, that Parliament was dissolved, and for more than ten years (1629 to 1640) the King carried on government without it.

§ 24. **Ship Money.**—A few years afterwards (1634) a writ for ship money was drawn up by Noy, the Attorney-General, who, in doing so, carefully followed the ancient precedents, which went back to the time of the Plantagenets and the Conquest. This writ was addressed to the *maritime* towns, seaports, and counties on the pretext of defending the coast against pirates; and this first request for ship money was, on the whole, fairly well received. Next year, however, a second writ was issued by which the *inland* towns and counties were included, and to this there was much opposition. Charles, however, obtained from ten of the judges the opinion that the levy of ship money from all counties was lawful (December, 1635), and a third, fourth, and fifth writ were issued in following years. As everyone knows, this tax was vigorously resisted by John Hampden in the Law Courts, and also by Pym and Granville in the Short Parliament. Finally, when the Long Parliament met, the levy of ship money was pronounced illegal by a bill to which the King had to give his assent (1641). Only a year after this Charles set up his standard at Nottingham, and the war between King and Parliament began. Of that war we need not here speak further, but must proceed to the commercial history of the period in which it was waged.

CHAPTER VI.

COMMERCE IN THE 17TH CENTURY.

§ 25. **Increase of Foreign Commerce.**—We now come to a rather troubled period in English history, through which, however, the development of commerce, in spite of obstacles caused by internal disputes, continued to progress steadily. From the time when Charles I. began to reign, to the breaking out of the war between him and the Parliament, to which we have alluded at the end of the last chapter, the progress not only of commerce but of colonisation was very clearly marked. We have already seen how our American and West Indian colonies were founded, and now we notice that the West Indies especially were about this time taken possession of and settled by Englishmen. St. Christopher, Nevis, the Carribbee Islands, the Barbadoes, and the Bahamas, all owe their plantation, more or less, to this period; and so also does the colony of Surinam in South America (1641). This process of colonisation was at the same time both a cause and a sign of the general increase of our foreign trade, while the extent and variety of this trade is testified by a contemporary writer, Lewis Roberts, in his work entitled *The Merchant's Map of Commerce* (1638), wherein he speaks in the

COMMERCE IN THE 17TH CENTURY. 33

following glowing terms of the prosperity of England: "When I survey every kingdom and great city of the world, and every petty port and creek of the same, and find in each of these some English prying after the trade and commerce thereof, then am I easily brought to imagine that either this great traffic of England is at its full perfection, or that it aims higher than can, hitherto, by my weak sight be either seen or discovered." He further remarks that English commerce was now no longer confined to the export of the staple merchandise of the country—such as cloth, lead, tin, and drapery—but that we had obtained a fairly considerable carrying trade as well, so that other nations now obtained the products of distant foreign countries through the agency of English merchants. For example, the East Indian Company now had the traffic with India, Arabia, and Persia, of which the Italian merchants had formerly the monopoly. In the same way the Levant Company now carried on nearly all the traffic with Turkish and Asiatic ports which formerly had been in the hands of France. These and other details serve to show that England was now beginning to take her place in the first rank of commercial nations.

§ 26. **Prosperity at Home: General Post and Growth of London.**—At home the same activity and prosperity is shown by several facts which we may mention in this place. Foremost, perhaps, among them, was the opening of the *Royal* Post to the public.[1] James I. had made beginnings in this direction, but the real origin of the Post-office dates only from Charles's reign; for, hitherto, the intercourse between various parts of the country, and especially between England and Scotland, had been quite

[1] The Post was given out in farm as a monopoly up to 1678. *Cf.* *Economic Journal*, iii., pp. 443 *sqq.*

irregular. It was now, however, arranged that a post should run between Edinburgh and London, "to go thither and come back in six days," while branch posts were arranged in connection with this main route in order to carry letters to and from other important towns. The General Post-office for the three kingdoms was only established in 1656. These posts were carried on horseback, but we may mention, in passing, that hackney-coaches, another sign of growing prosperity, first came into prominence in London in Charles's reign. Moreover, the continuous and rapid growth of London itself, and the rapid building of houses therein, was another sign of increasing wealth. In fact, so rapid was the increase of the capital, that sovereigns became frightened at its size, and both James I. and Charles I. issued repeated proclamations [1] with a view of checking it, chiefly upon the grounds that a large number of the nobility and gentry were drawn away from the country and took to residing in London, to the great impoverishing of their estates. We may also mention in this connection that some time before this the water supply of the capital had been found so insufficient that it became necessary to increase it by bringing what is still called the New River (1609), to Clerkenwell, which feat was accomplished under the superintendence of Hugh Middleton.

§ 27. **Distribution of Wealth in the Country.**—But not only London, but other parts of the country, were also in an increasingly prosperous condition, and a very good estimate of the general wealth of the nation outside London may be formed from taking the figures of the assessment of ship money that was made in 1636 for England

---

[1] Elizabeth had issued similar proclamations.

and Wales. The following table will show clearly which were the richest counties :—

Name of County.	Assessment per Square Mile.
Middlesex (including London)	£7
North Hants, Bedford, Buckingham, Hertford, and Berks, Kent	£6—£7
Suffolk, Essex, Surrey, Dorset, Wilts, Somerset, Worcestershire, Warwick, Leicester	£5—£6
Cornwall, Hants, Oxon, Gloucester, Shrops, Hereford, Notts, Cambridge	£4—£5
Sussex, Devon, Norfolk, Monmouth, Cheshire, Derby, Lincoln	£3—£4
Stafford, Yorks, Wales	£2—£3
Lancashire, Westmoreland, Durham, Northumberland, Cumberland	Under £2

In this table it will be seen that Middlesex (including London) naturally heads the list; then come the home and Midland Counties, whilst Staffordshire, Yorkshire, Lancashire, and the north, were still comparatively poor. These latter counties remained behind the rest of England until the Industrial Revolution at the close of the 18th century.

§ 28. **The Civil War: Growth of Banking.**—Naturally, the Civil War which raged for so many years between the King and Parliament caused some depression both to home and foreign trade, but, nevertheless, the confusion excited by it seems not to have been so marked as we might expect.[1]

[1] Cf. Thorold Rogers, *Six Centuries of Work and Wages*, ch. xvi.; and Cunningham, *Growth of English Industry and Commerce*, ii., 102, § 198.

And as soon as the Commonwealth Government was firmly established, the prosperity of the country continued to increase as steadily as ever. In fact, some say that during the Commonwealth period trade advanced more than it had ever done before. The well-known writer, Sir Josiah Child, to whom we shall refer later, declared that between 1650 and 1670 the number of merchants and shipping had doubled; while another authority, Sir William Petty, states that the value of houses in London (and in many other towns also) was doubled between 1636 and 1676.

Certainly a sure sign of the increase of national wealth is to be found in the growth of Banking as an institution, and upon this subject we have very accurate information from a pamphlet, of 1676, called *The Mystery of the New-fashioned Goldsmiths or Bankers Discovered.* In previous times London merchants had often kept their cash in the Royal Mint in the Tower, but when Charles I., shortly before the meeting of the Long Parliament, seized £200,000 of the deposits there, under the pretext of a loan, it was felt that even the Tower afforded no longer much security. Hence, we are told, it became the custom about the year 1645 for merchants and men of business to place their cash in the hands of goldsmiths, and this new banking business soon grew very considerably, since the goldsmiths combined the callings of money-lenders, discounters of merchants' bills, and estate agents. The consequence was that this new business quickly brought a great quantity of cash into their hands, so that the greatest amongst them were enabled to supply Cromwell with money in advance, upon security of revenue, "as his occasions required, upon great advantages to themselves," as may be well supposed.

After the Restoration, the goldsmiths continued to have

financial dealings with the Government, but to their cost they found that Charles II. was by no means a trustworthy debtor. In 1672 that gay monarch's debts were so large that he resorted to the expedient of robbery. He had in his treasury about £1,300,000 of money which he had borrowed from the goldsmiths at 12 per cent., upon the security of the taxes, but instead of repaying it when the taxes came in, he announced that the taxes should be devoted, not to the repayment of his debts, but to the war with the Dutch; while, in addition to this loss, the lenders had their interest reduced from 12 to 6 per cent. Naturally, a great commercial crisis followed, and many goldsmiths, as well as merchants who had banked with them, were ruined. Nevertheless the system of banking with goldsmiths continued in operation for many years longer.

Here, therefore, we see the origin and rapid growth of our present banking system, which, towards the close of the 17th century, was to receive a new stimulus from the foundation of the Bank of England.

§ 29. **Colonial Trade.**—Our woollen trade continued in a very satisfactory condition during all the time of the Commonwealth. About the year 1651 the company of Merchant Adventurers who chiefly carried on this trade removed their staple from Dort to Hamburg, which port soon became the sole staple[1] for the English woollen trade. This shows a considerable increase in our manufacturing industries at home; but even more significant than this, perhaps, was the steady growth of our new colonial settlements. It was the West Indies especially that came into prominence at this time by the introduction of sugar canes from Brazil, and the sugar industry made the fortune of many a colonial planter. The author of *Trade Revived* (1659) speaks of Barbadoes

[1] See the author's *Industry in England*, pp. 135-137, for explanation of the staple system.

as giving to "many men of low degree vast fortunes equal to those of noblemen." There is also no doubt that the capture of Jamaica by Cromwell from the Spaniards (1655) greatly helped the development of our commerce as well as our political power in the West Indies. The trade with our American plantations was also increasing rapidly, and was entirely in our own hands. Sir William Petty, writing in 1676, mentions that above 40,000 tons of shipping (at that time a considerable quantity) was employed in the Guinea and American trade, which in former times had been inconsiderable. And if we anticipate the order of events a little, we may also quote the authority of Davenant upon this subject, who tells us that the exports of the North American plantation trade rose to an average value of about £350,000 in the six years 1682 to 1688, while the imports therefrom were reckoned about £950,000, of which the greater part was re-exported from England to continental countries.[1]

§ 30. **The Navigation Acts.**—Still, with all this prosperity the Englishmen of Cromwell's day were not quite satisfied. Although, as we have said, British merchants were obtaining a fair share in the carrying trade of the world, the Dutch were still the foremost nation in that respect, and were the ocean carriers of that day both to the East and West. Hence English statesmen thought it necessary to pass the famous Navigation Acts of 1651, which were subsequently renewed and enlarged in 1672. These Acts forbade the importation of goods from Asia, Africa, or America in any but English vessels or ships of the country where

[1] The chief *exports to* America were provisions, apparel, household furniture. *Imports from* America, tobacco, sugar, ginger, cotton, dyes, cocoa, fish, and fur.

these goods were made.[1] They were aimed directly at the Dutch, and this nation was not long in resenting them. The year after they were passed a naval war broke out between the Dutch and English, which, though only of short duration (1652 to 1654), was by no means the last of the various struggles caused by the commercial rivalry of these two nations. It has been often assumed that these Acts greatly increased our commercial prosperity, and ultimately gave us that supremacy which we now enjoy. But this may be doubted. That supremacy was due, not to one, but to many causes, and it is very probable that our wars with the Dutch took away much of the profits that we gained from the Acts which caused them.

§ 31. **Evidences of Prosperity.**—It is, however, on the whole certain (though some contemporary authorities seem to point to a different conclusion) that our prosperity at this time was steady and continuous, as may be seen from the Custom House records from the year 1613 to 1669. They may be exhibited by taking three single years as specimens :—

Year.	Exports and Imports together.
1613	£4,628,586
1622	£4,939,751
1669	£6,259,413

[1] More fully the Acts enacted that no merchandise, either of Asia, Africa, or America, except only such as should be imported directly from the place of its growth or manufactured in Europe, should be imported into England, Ireland, or any of the plantations, in any but English built ships belonging either to English or English plantation

It is noticeable also how quickly London was rebuilt after the great fire of 1666; for the speedy and costly rebuilding of the capital after that great conflagration was, as Sir Josiah Child remarks, a convincing and indeed amazing argument of the plenty and increase of money in England.

This writer whom we have just quoted also gives us many other details of the state of commerce at this time in his *New Discourse on Trade*, published in 1690, and written[1] at his country house during the Great Plague. In this he points out that our foreign trade had not only increased, but had also changed its direction in several cases. The most extensive increase was with Spain, Portugal, and the East Indies, though in the East the Dutch were as usual still ahead of us, carrying on a trade with China and Japan in which the English had no share at all. The general commerce of the country, though it had declined in some directions, had increased in others, and was never before so extensive or so profitable. Besides the countries just mentioned, our trade with Turkey and Italy was more active than at any other time, and our American plantations were becoming more and more important to us. These statements are confirmed by Petty (whom we have already quoted), who mentions especially the great increase of houses in towns like Newcastle, Yarmouth, Norwich, Exeter, and

subjects, navigated by English commanders, and having at least three-fourths of the sailors Englishmen. It was also further enacted that no goods, growth, production, or manufacture of any country in Europe should be imported into Great Britain except in British ships or in such ships as were the real property of the people of the country or place in which the goods were produced or from which they could only be or most usually were exported.

[1] A first draft of the book was published under another title as early as 1668.

Portsmouth, and declares that the revenue of the Crown was treble what it had been forty years previously. The most complete information on this subject is given us by Davenant in his *Discourses on Trade* (1698), who estimated that the rental of the kingdom had risen from about £6,000,000 per annum in 1600, to £14,000,000 in 1688; that the mercantile shipping was nearly double what it had been twenty years previously; while the general wealth of the country had more than doubled itself twice over between 1600 and 1688.

§ 32. **The Huguenot Immigrants.**—To swell the tide of our prosperity, we now received upon our shores, owing to the Revocation of the Edict of Nantes in 1685, a large number of foreign workmen who possessed not only skill but capital wherewith to develop old industries, or to introduce new ones. The Huguenots who fled from the bigotry of the French king, Louis XIV., numbered hundreds of thousands, and they escaped to many countries of Europe. It is said by a high authority [1] that at least 50,000 of them came to Great Britain, and brought three million pounds' worth of capital with them. An entire suburb of London was peopled with French manufacturers of silk, while others carried to England the arts of making glass, hats, and paper, which had hitherto been rather backward amongst us. Their descendants are now to be found in all parts of England, and they have contributed in many ways to the moral and material welfare of the country of their adoption.

We now come to the close of the 17th century, which we have seen to be a period of considerable development. Even the great revolution of 1688, although it brought in

[1] Anderson, *Chron. Deduct. Commerce*, ii. 181 (ed. 1764).

its train various financial difficulties, was not a serious bar to progress; on the contrary, the period just succeeding it was marked by the foundation of some of the most important institutions in the whole of our commercial history. Of these we shall speak in the next chapter.

CHAPTER VII.

COMMERCIAL INSTITUTIONS AND LEGISLATION UNDER WILLIAM III.

§ 33. **The Revolution, the National Debt, and the Bank of England.**—The Revolution of 1688, which drove the Stuarts from the throne of England, was accomplished (as far as home affairs were concerned) with comparatively little bloodshed. But it led to a series of wars with France which placed William III. in severe pecuniary difficulties, and among other things utterly destroyed a flourishing trade with France that had sprung up in the days of James II. But even these wars were by no means fatal to our home and foreign industry, and Davenant remarks that, notwithstanding all that England suffered, the country still had the principle of life strong within it, and that from the manner in which it had stood the severe strain of the war, great hopes might be entertained for the future. As a matter of fact, his hopes were fully justified, for the first few years after William III.'s accession saw the rise of two great institutions, the Bank of England and the National Debt, as well as the complete and much needed restoration of the currency. We will speak first of the National Debt. It was then a new scheme, which was rendered necessary by the fact that the current revenue was insufficient to meet the expenses of our French wars,

[1] These institutions were largely imitated from the Dutch.

and because the King and his ministers—representing as they did a new dynasty not yet firmly established in the affections of the people—dared not render themselves unpopular by imposing any fresh taxes.

Moreover, the revenue was now fixed at £1,200,000 a year, the same figure as was arranged at the Restoration; and William, much to his disappointment, was left with only about £800,000 free of parliamentary control.[1] About £600,000 more was granted from the Customs, but only for four years; consequently some scheme was necessary by which an increase of taxation might be avoided, while at the same time the necessary funds for the prosecution of the war should be forthcoming. In 1692, Montagu, Chancellor of the Exchequer, succeeded in borrowing from various subscribers one million sterling, the interest of which was secured by new duties on liquors. This was the beginning of the National Debt.[2] But the sum thus raised was found to be insufficient, and next year another loan was raised, this time in the form of the capital of the new Bank of England. Montagu borrowed £1,200,000 at 8 per cent., and the subscribers of this sum were formed into a company, who considered the loan made to the Government as part of their capital, while the interest upon it was secured by the taxes. Their charter was granted to them at first for eleven years only, the government of the company being placed in the

[1] This was henceforth known as the Civil List.

[2] At the death of William III. in 1702 the total amount of the debt was £16,394,000, which represents the cost of our continental wars during his reign. From 1702 it continued to increase, till at the beginning of our war with the American colonies it had risen to £128,583,636. The American War cost over £121,000,000. At the beginning of the war with France in 1793 the National Debt stood at about £239,000,000; and at its termination in 1815 it was about £876,000,000.

hands of a governor, deputy-governor, and 24 directors. The new bank was allowed to trade only in bullion, bills of exchange, and forfeited pledges, and it is a sign of the jealous regard to National interests shown by the Parliament of that time, that a proviso was made that the bank should not lend money to the Crown without the consent of Parliament. At first there was a great deal of opposition to the bank that had thus been formed, the opposition coming naturally from the goldsmiths, whose occupation as bankers, to which we have alluded, seemed now to be threatened by a formidable rival. They even attempted to destroy the new institution by buying up all its paper and then suddenly demanding immediate payment. The directors of the bank, however, gained time by referring their hasty creditors to the law courts, and during the delay thus gained restored their credit by extensive calls upon their subscribers. Just about this time their position was much improved by the fall of their rival, the Land Bank,[1] which had for a short time enjoyed much popularity, and had at first seriously threatened the operations of the Bank of England. After this time the existence and prosperity of the bank was assured, and it rapidly became, what it now is, our greatest financial institution.

§ 34. **The Land Tax.**—The financial difficulties of the new Government were, however, not yet at an end, and

---

[1] This was a bank formed to lend money upon landed security, the idea being that everyone who had real property ought besides to have paper money to the full value of their property. There were, indeed, various projects for banks and other commercial enterprises afloat about this time, and the period between 1692 and 1696 was also one of considerable speculation and severe commercial crises; cf. Cunningham, ii., 394-399.

it was found necessary to raise money by means of the Land Tax, or rather by making a new valuation of the land and re-imposing the former tax. The Land Tax had been used as a means of raising revenue in 1625, and also in Charles II.'s reign. It was really a general tax[1] of 4s. in the £ upon property, but those whose lands were not worth 20s. a year were not taxed, and the lands at first were rated very low. But now, in 1692, the land of the country was regularly valued, and after that time varying amounts in the £ were charged in different years, and the tax was voted annually, until 1798, when it was made permanent at 4s. in the £. Landowners were permitted, however, to redeem the tax by a single payment. Since 1798 a great part of it has been redeemed in this way, and at present only one per cent. of the revenue comes from this source.

§ 35. **Restoration of the Currency and of National Credit.**—One of the first operations of the new Bank of England was to help the Government in the issue of a new currency. About the end of the reign of Charles II., and still more in that of James II., great inconvenience had begun to be felt from the clipping of silver money so much practised at this time, for the old silver coinage was not milled at the edges, and thus any clippings taken off it were not easily discovered. At first an attempt was made to issue good silver whilst the old debased coins were still in circulation, but this was found to be of no use, and therefore it was decided to call in the whole amount of clipped silver money then in circulation, and to issue a completely new coinage. It was then found that the depreciation amounted to about 5s. in every 11s., so that

[1] Cf. Cunningham, ii., 405.
[2] For §§ 33, 34, 35, students might consult Macaulay's *History*.

the whole £4,000,000 of clipped money that was brought in was therefore not worth much more than £2,000,000 sterling. Consequently there was a great loss upon the recoinage, the expenses of which had to be defrayed by a tax on windows, while the old money was accepted in payment of taxes. The new coinage was carefully milled, and was issued under the supervision of Sir Isaac Newton, who was then Warden[1] of the Mint (1696). This great measure, which involved financial operations of some difficulty, did a great deal to restore public credit, which was still further strengthened by the passing of three resolutions by Parliament, to the effect that : (1) The Commons would assist the King to prosecute the war with France with all possible energy; (2) that in no case should the value of the new coinage be changed; and (3) that Parliament would pledge itself to make good the deficiency in the funds voted in 1695. There is no doubt that the passing of these resolutions, combined with the sound financial operations involved in the foundation of the Bank of England, the creating of the National Debt, and the issue of the new currency, did a great deal not only to restore confidence among the commercial classes and all others at home, but also to enhance the credit and importance of England in the eyes of the nations of Europe. Not long after this, Louis XIV., evidently seeing that England was by no means in so impoverished a condition as he had expected, determined to conclude the war with William III. in which he had been engaged, and the Peace of Ryswick was arranged between the combatants in 1697.

This treaty is important, because by it Louis XIV. (then the leading monarch in Europe) agreed to recognise as

[1] He became "Master" only in 1699.

legal the succession of William III., and after him of Anne, to the English throne, and thus admitted the hopelessness of the cause of the Stuarts whom he had so warmly supported. We should not, finally, leave this period without a grateful recognition of the services of two men who deserve to be specially mentioned in connection with the economic development of their country. They were Charles Montagu, Chancellor of the Exchequer, afterwards Earl of Halifax, and William Paterson, the real founder of the Bank of England.

§ 36. **Commerce Flourishing: The Board of Trade.** —With financial affairs at home thus placed upon a satisfactory basis, it is not astonishing to find that our commerce abroad continued to thrive in spite of the troubles caused by the war with France. We shall speak in another chapter of the development of, and the opposition to, the East India Company, and of the growth of our American colonies, as these two subjects are important enough to deserve special treatment for themselves. It is sufficient to say here that the plantations or settlements in America were steadily increasing in population and wealth, and by the end of the 17th century our trade with these colonies and the West Indies was giving employment to no less than 500 ships. The fisheries of Newfoundland were also important, though even at that period the French were giving trouble by claiming fishing rights off the Newfoundland banks. On the other hand, the Greenland whale fisheries were by no means successful, and a company that was started for carrying them on in 1692 was, after a few years, compelled to abandon their enterprise. But with slight exceptions like this our general traffic was in the most flourishing condition, and it became sufficiently important for the formation of a permanent Board of Trade. Such an institution had already been founded[1] by Charles II. in 1660, but it was only kept up for five or six years. But in 1695 King William appointed a regular board, consisting of a First Lord and seven Commissioners, entitled "The Commissioners for Promoting the Trade of this Kingdom and for Inspecting and Improving the Plantations in America and elsewhere." Their chief business was "to consider by what means already existing manufactures might be improved, or new manufactures introduced, and to superintend the commerce and government of the plantations and colonies." This latter duty of looking after the colonies was taken from it upon the institution of the post of Secretary of State for the Colonies in the next century (1768), but its other duties remained pretty much the same until the abolition of the "Commission" in 1782, when its business was handed over to a permanent committee of the Privy Council. In 1786 the Board of Trade, with substantially the same functions as at present, was established by an order in Council.

§ 37. **The Woollen Industry and the Corn Laws.**
—Of the whole trade of the country which this board was supposed to look after, the most important branch at this time was the woollen trade. Wool and woollen goods had now long since become, and for a long time afterwards remained, our chief article of produce and export; and in the reign of William III. its manufacture was regulated in various ways. An Act of 1698 (9 William III., c. 40) declares that "The wool and woollen manu-

[1] Cromwell had originated the idea also in 1655 when what was apparently a temporary Commission was appointed. (Thurloe, *State Papers*, iv. 177.)

factures of cloth, serge, baize, kerseys, and other stuffs made or mixed with wool, are the greatest and most profitable commodities of this kingdom on which the value of lands and the trade of the nation do chiefly depend;" and so afraid were English manufacturers that their great staple should pass into other hands, that Ireland and the American colonies were strictly prohibited from exporting wool or woollen goods to any part of the world excepting to England.[1] Davenant, whom we have already quoted, estimated the value of wool yearly shorn in England at the close of the 17th century at £2,000,000, and the value of our manufacture at about £8,000,000, of which about a quarter was exported. These figures may, perhaps, be exaggerated, but in any case they give us a very fair idea of the importance of the industry at this period. It must not be forgotten also that England was a great wool growing as well as wool manufacturing country, and that our manufactures then by no means assumed the great preponderance over the agricultural interest which they now possess. In fact, the agricultural interest was at that time the most powerful in England; and a proof of its power may be seen in the regulations which were made, immediately after the Revolution of 1688, in favour of the corn-growers—that is to say, the farmers and great landowners of the country. For a long time past the export and import of corn had been the subject of many Acts, and in 1670 a law was passed by which corn could not be brought from abroad till the price at home rose to 53s. 4d. per quarter, though it might be exported perfectly free. This,

[1] English growers also were forbidden to export wool, so that all wool grown in England might be manufactured in the country; see further, Adam Smith, *Wealth of Nations*, Bk. iv., ch. 8.

however, was thought by the agricultural interest not to be sufficient protection, and therefore by the Act 1 William and Mary, c. 12, corn-growers were positively paid to send their produce out of the country, and the importation of corn was almost prohibited. In other words, a bounty of 5s. per quarter was allowed on every quarter of wheat exported, as long as the price of the home market did not exceed 48s.; and all exported corn was relieved even from Custom House duties, while imported corn was subjected to the same heavy duties as before. No doubt the landowners who got this law passed did not quite realise what severe harm it would do the nation in later years; but, nevertheless, the whole subject of Corn Law legislation is a striking instance of what human avarice is capable when it is unchecked by any adequate interference with its tendencies.[1]

[1] Cf. *Wealth of Nations*, Bk. iv., ch. 5: *Digression on the Corn Laws.*

CHAPTER VIII.

THE METHUEN TREATY AND THE UNION OF SCOTLAND
WITH ENGLAND.

§ 38. **Shipping and Export Trade.** — On the whole we may regard the reign of William III. as being very prosperous for English commerce. It is true that owing to the circumstances under which he came to the throne he was for most of his time engaged in war, but that war was carried on abroad, and the wealth of the country was sufficient to pay for it without letting it interrupt the course of our home and foreign trade to any great extent. Even whilst it was going on, trade and manufactures flourished greatly. There was a great demand for labour, and it is stated by Chalmers that the foreign traffic and navigation of England was doubled during the period from the Peace of Ryswick to the accession of Queen Anne. Certainly our foreign trade, if measured by the extent of our shipping, must have made considerable progress. At the end of the reign of William (January 1702), the number of vessels belonging to all the ports of England was 3281, but the total tonnage was 261,222 tons, which is nearly 80 tons on the average, and the total number of seamen was 27,196.[1] If we add to the mercantile marine the sailors of the Navy as well, it seems

[1] Cf. Craik's *Hist. of Brit. Commerce*, ii. 169.

probable that there were above 70,000 seamen in all. We only mention this as one proof of the general extent of our shipping and foreign commerce, but it will be easily understood that the re-coinage of silver, and the Acts passed for supporting public credit, coupled with the new methods of finance which were now instituted, all helped to invigorate and strengthen the trade of the country. It is also noticeable that during the whole of William's reign many foreign merchants and workmen came and settled in England, finding shelter from the religious persecutions raging in less tolerant countries, as is proved by the many Acts of naturalisation which were passed in every session of Parliament at this time.

The progress thus made in William's reign did not stop in that of Queen Anne, although here again the operations of war continued during nearly the whole of her reign. Our exports were continually rising in value from 1705 to 1713, as may be seen from the following table:—

Year.	Exports.
1705	£5,308,966
1709	£5,913,357
1711	£5,962,988
1712	£6,868,840
1713 1714 1715	average £7,696,573

§ 39. **The Methuen Treaty.**—At this point a commercial treaty was made that had important consequences in certain branches of our foreign commerce. This famous treaty is known as the Methuen Treaty of 1703 because it was arranged by John Methuen, the English ambassador to Portugal. It has been called "the bribe offered to Portugal to join the Grand Alliance," because certain commercial advantages were offered to her if she would do so. The treaty was inspired by the jealousy of France which, not unnaturally, had long existed in the minds of English traders, and which was accentuated by the manner in which France had always helped the Stuart cause. It was hoped that by this treaty France would be injured in so far as one fruitful source of wealth, namely her wine trade with us, would be almost cut off. Therefore it was arranged that the Portuguese were no longer to prohibit the importation of English woollen cloths and other goods into their country, but were to admit them to their markets, while in return for this privilege the wines of Portugal were to be admitted to England at two-thirds of the duty payable on the wines of France. The result was a considerable increase of trade with Portugal, but an even greater decrease of trade with France. At the same time the wine-drinking of the richer classes in England took a very different direction; for port, which had hitherto been unknown in England, became now the typical drink of the English gentleman, and more port was sent to the United Kingdom than to all the rest of Europe put together. The Methuen Treaty was maintained till 1831, and the heavy duties on French wines were not reduced[1] till 1860. As this treaty was based upon a mutual monopoly, it was almost sure to be injurious to one or both of the two parties contracting it. As far as we can see, Portugal, though she gained by it in politics, was almost driven out of her own market in her colony of Brazil by English merchants who sent their manufactures

[1] Except for a short time under the Eden Treaty of 1786 (p. 93).

THE METHUEN TREATY. 55

there as well as to Portugal, and she also was induced to devote to the production of wine a far larger amount of capital than she would otherwise have done, and consequently never developed her home manufactures as much as might otherwise have been the case. England also lost nearly all her trade with France, and though this was partly compensated by the increase of trade to Portugal and Brazil, it may be doubted whether even then we got the full value for the price which we paid for this treaty.[1] At the time, however, the treaty was thought to be a masterpiece of commercial diplomacy; and after all, we should not be too severe in judging it, for the general economic ideas of that age must be taken into account, and it is not very long since we ourselves have learned a fuller wisdom.

§ 40. **The Union between England and Scotland: The Darien Scheme.**—Besides this important treaty with a foreign power, the reign of Queen Anne is noticeable for another treaty which took place with a country much nearer home. We refer to the Act of Union between England and Scotland. The Union between these two countries had for some time been desired by the more far-seeing among English and Scotch politicians and men of business, of whom the celebrated William Paterson was one. Men were beginning to see that it was almost ridiculous that two countries which were united under the same sovereign, and whose interests were in many respects so closely allied, were yet for all intents and purposes as much cut off one from the other as if they were two

---

[1] See my *Commerce in Europe*, paragraph 116. It should also be added, as Prof. C. F. Bastable remarks, that the hope of obtaining the precious metals directly from the producer (in this case, Portugal) was one of the motives of the Treaty.

separate kingdoms. This was especially felt to be the case in matters of commerce, and circumstances which had recently occurred in Scotland made many Scotchmen feel that it was desirable to become commercially an integral part of England. Chief among these circumstances was the terrible failure of what is known as the Darien Scheme. This was a project originated by William Paterson, who proposed to colonise the Isthmus of Darien, and use it as "the key to the Indies and door of the world" for commerce. English capitalists, however, would not support his scheme, and it was denounced by the English Parliament. Nevertheless, a company was formed in Scotland called the "Scottish African and Indian Company," to which a charter was given by the Scotch Parliament in 1695, and a capital of £900,000 was with some difficulty ultimately raised. Of this capital, only £400,000 came from Scotland (which was then a very poor country), and the rest from various English and Dutch merchants. But powerful influences were against the new scheme. The East India Company, the Levant Company, and the Dutch merchants in general never ceased to oppose it, and it was owing to their influence that when the ill-fated colony at last set out for Darien in July, 1698, the settlers were left quite unaided against the attacks of the Spaniards. This nation at that time claimed the monopoly of the South American trade, and declared that the new company was infringing it. What with the attacks of the Spaniards, and the climate, which was totally unsuitable for Europeans, the expedition was doomed to failure. In fact, few of its members ever returned.

This failure had the most serious effect in impoverishing the Scotch, who could then ill afford the loss, but there

THE METHUEN TREATY. 57

is little doubt that it greatly helped to bring about the subsequent Act of Union in 1707, wherein William Paterson was largely concerned. The clauses of the Act which interest us from the commercial point of view are the 2nd and 3rd, by which it was arranged that £398,000 were to be paid by England to Scotland, in order to pay off the Scotch debt and indemnify the shareholders in the Darien Company, and that the Scotch were not to pay any of the terminable taxes which had been granted by the English Parliament. Trade and commercial intercourse between the two countries were to be entirely free, and Scotland was admitted as a sharer in every department of English commerce, even in the plantations and colonies. The chief benefit of the Union to England was merely the increase of trade generally with Scotland; but Scotland gained a great deal more, for she found a large market for woollen and linen goods and cattle, not only in England, but in America, and received much advantage from the substitution of the new English currency for her own depreciated coins. The benefit, however, was not altogether one-sided, for the energy and intellect of the Scotch have contributed not a little to the national greatness of the United Kingdom, and to national success in many commercial and financial enterprises.

CHAPTER IX.

THE TREATY OF UTRECHT AND THE SOUTH SEA BUBBLE.

§ 41. **War with Louis XIV.**—During most of this time England was still engaged in the struggles of a continental war, for after the deposition of James II., war had been rendered necessary by the tremendous power of France under Louis XIV. William III. saw that it was inevitable for the interests of England that Louis XIV. should be checked, and the War of the Spanish Succession (1702 to 1713) was carried on with the object of preventing that king from adding the resources of Spain to those of his own kingdom. If he had done so, two disastrous results would have happened: the Stuarts would by his help have been restored to the English throne, and the struggle against absolute monarchy and religious tyranny would probably have been fought over again; and, secondly, the growth of English commerce would have been checked, if not utterly ruined, by the preservation of the Spanish and French monopoly of the Western world; for at that time Spain and France between them possessed nearly all the explored portion of North and South America. But, as it happened, England succeeded in avoiding both these results, and when the war was finally over in 1713, we found ourselves by the Treaty of Utrecht in possession of Gibraltar, now one of the keys of our Indian Empire, and of the Hudson's

Bay territory, Newfoundland, and Nova Scotia, the foundations of our present Canadian dominion. At the same time, although Philip of France, the grandson of Louis XIV., was to be king of Spain, the crowns of France and Spain were never to be united, and France was compelled to acknowledge the Protestant Succession of the House of Hanover in England. Moreover, the English were to have the right of trading in slaves to America, and of sending one ship a year to the South Seas. During all these wars, as we have seen, our trade had been expanding, and though there was a slight depression in our foreign commerce at the accession of George I., there seems to have been no real check to our national industries, for the demands of the home market seemed to have been so great as to counterbalance, even if they did not partially cause, the decline in foreign trade.

§ 42. **The South Sea Mania.**—The same story of progress is seen in the reign of George I., and no surer proof of this can be found than the fact that this period was distinguished by that mania for new projects which found its climax and its destruction in the now famous South Sea Bubble. So far from showing an unhealthy condition of our trade and industry, this "bubble," as it is called, and the many other schemes with which it was accompanied, were a sure sign of the fact that people had rather more capital than they knew what to do with. It should also be remembered that the South Sea Bubble was only one of a large number of similar schemes, and though we mention it prominently because it has always been spoken about as a great event in English history, it is well to emphasise the fact that it was only one scheme amongst many others, and probably caused less ruin in the end than some of the less known company manias. This company had been formed in 1711 with a view of saving the State part of the 8 per cent. interest which had been paid them upon the floating debit of £10,000,000. The company took over the debt, and only asked 6 per cent. from the State; while in return the Government granted them the monopoly [1] of the trade with the Pacific and East Coast of South America, about the wealth of which regions fabulous legends were current. The affairs of the company flourished considerably till 1720, when an arrangement was made with the Government to lessen once more the interest of 6 per cent. upon the National Debt, which was then about £31,000,000. The South Sea Company was to take over the Government debt, and to accept only 5 per cent. interest; while the creditors of the Government were to exchange their 6 per cent. bonds for 4 per cent. shares in the company, with a prospect of sharing in the profits of the company's trade. So strong was the belief in the great profits of the South Sea trade, that the creditors of the Government were positively eager to transfer their debt from the State to the company; while the company itself, feeling the advantage of having a regular income of 5 per cent. secured by the State, was willing to pay no less than $3\frac{1}{2}$ millions to the State for permission to carry out this scheme. When the Bank of England made a rival offer, the South Sea Company gave no less than $7\frac{1}{2}$ millions for this permission. The net result was that the State paid 5 instead of 6 per cent., and obtained also the $7\frac{1}{2}$ millions just mentioned; the company

[1] Similarly in Law's famous Mississippi scheme, from which the projectors of the South Sea Company had taken the hint, it was the exclusive trade to Louisiana from which Law promised gigantic profits to French investors; cf. my *Commerce in Europe*, p. 160.

received a certain 5 per cent. from the State, and paid only 4 per cent. to the creditors, while the creditors lost 2 per cent., but had a chance of a share in the company's profits.[1] If things had remained thus, not much harm would have been done to anybody; but at the worst, if no profits were made, the creditors would only have lost 2 per cent. But so great was the belief in the large profits that would be derived, that the South Sea Company's shares rose to an enormous premium, till £100 shares came to sell at last for £1000 each. It is often forgotten, however, that the shares of other companies rose in a similar manner, though none rose quite as high as the South Sea Company; while hundreds of bogus companies were started for carrying out schemes of the most wild and visionary nature. To illustrate the credulity of people, and the mania for speculation at that day, it may be mentioned that one enterprising individual advertised a company with no definite aim, but simply "for some purpose hereafter to be declared," and actually found shareholders foolish enough to pay a deposit on the shares in a company of which they did not even know the object.[2] Strange to say, it was the South Sea Company itself that began its own downfall, by causing the Government to issue a writ against some of these bogus companies, and "against all other projects promulgated contrary to law." The result was a sudden panic; the shares of numerous companies fell rapidly, and amongst them those of the South Sea Company itself, and naturally the fall in the prices of shares brought ruin in its train. But the fact that the South Sea stock did not fall lower than £135 shows that the company was not only

[1] Cf. Airy's *Hist. of Eng.*, p. 360.
[2] See Anderson, *Chrono. Deduct. of Commerce*, ii. 295.

solvent, but even prosperous. Nevertheless, a fierce clamour rose against the directors of the company, and they were obliged to lay a full account before the House of Commons, and to state the value of their estates, while a secret committee of inquiry was appointed. In the end the directors were disabled from taking office or sitting in Parliament, and their whole estates were confiscated; only a small allowance being given to save them from beggary. This was the occasion when Walpole came prominently before the nation as a financier, although even before this time his skill in that direction had been known. In February, 1721, he made an arrangement by which the State remitted the $7\frac{1}{2}$ millions promised by the company; the sums raised from the forfeited estates of the directors were applied to keeping up the credit of the company, and one-third of the capital invested in it was paid to the investors.[1]

§ 43. **Walpole's Ministry : Foreign War.**—Walpole now became First Lord of the Treasury and Prime Minister (March, 1721), and for twenty years longer he directed the political, commercial, and financial policy of the nation. As far as the history of commerce is concerned we owe him no small amount of gratitude, for during his long period of office peace was kept, the resources of the country were developed, and much encouragement was given to colonisation and colonial trade. Under his ministry was founded the colony of Georgia, which was the last of our settlements in America before the War of Independence.

But in spite of Walpole's persistent desire to maintain

[1] It might be added that the South Sea collapse was but one instance of the periodical crises which constantly occur in modern commerce.

peace, a time came when war once more broke out. It was due almost entirely to the growth of English commerce. " It happened that Spain, the weakest of European nations, had the most extended territory open to commercial enterprise. As in the days of Elizabeth, the Spanish Government tried to prevent the English from trading with its dominions, whilst the Spanish colonists, on the other hand, were anxious to promote a trade by which they were benefited. It was notorious that English merchants did their best to evade the restrictions imposed on them by the Treaty of Utrecht."[1] By that treaty they had been allowed to send annually to Panama only one ship of 600 tons to trade with the Spanish colonists (p. 59), but this regulation was evaded. The one ship sailed into the harbour and discharged its goods; but as soon as it was dark, smaller vessels, which had kept out of sight during the day-time, sailed in and filled it up again, so that this one ship was enabled to put many shiploads ashore. Besides this, there was an immense amount of smuggling carried on by Englishmen on various parts of the coast of Spanish America. In revenge the Spanish coastguards often seized English vessels suspected of smuggling, and sometimes ill-treated their crews. They also claimed the right of searching English vessels, even on the high seas, disputed the claim of the English to cut logwood on Campeachy Bay, and alleged that the new English colony of Georgia encroached on the boundaries of the Spanish territory of Florida. These formed, from the English point of view, sufficient grounds to declare war against Spain, although Walpole himself was much opposed to a conflict, and did not enter upon it till

[1] Cf. S. R. Gardiner, *Student's History of England*, ch. 46, p. 230, for this summary.

forced to do so by the clamours of William Pitt and the "patriots," who in 1738 brought forward a certain Captain Jenkins whose ear had been cut off by the Spanish coast-guards. His mutilation aroused much popular sympathy, and from this circumstance the war against Spain has been called " The War of Jenkins' Ear." This war merged into that of the Austrian Succession, in which France as usual helped Spain, these two nations being closely allied in The Family Compact. This war was concluded in 1748. Not long afterwards, however, another conflict, again caused by our mercantile and colonial expansion, broke out with France, and the Seven Years' War began in 1756. Its real causes are to be found in the French jealousy of our growing trade and possessions in India and North America; and of these we must now speak

CHAPTER X.

THE CONQUEST OF INDIA, A.D. 1600-1761.

§ 44. **The Factories of the East India Company.**—When we last heard of the East India Company it had only just begun its career as one among a number of similar companies, and by no means the greatest of these. It was doing a fairly considerable trade with India and the East Indies, though not so much as some people have imagined; but it had a great future before it, and circumstances, which no one could foresee, caused it to become not only a great commercial but also a great political power in the East.

Its history may be divided into three parts:[1] (1) The period of factories, 1612 to 1748; (2) the period of rivalry with France in Southern India, 1748 to 1761; and (3) the period of gradual conquest without European rivalry, 1761 to 1857.

The first of these periods is the longest, but contains the slowest progress of any of the three. It was a time when we had no territorial influence in India, but possessed merely factories or trading stations and depôts in various isolated districts. It should be remembered, by the way, that the first English factories were in Java, Sumatra, and other islands of the East Indies, from which, however, they were

[1] Cf. Caldecott's *Colonisation and Empire*, p. 60. He, however, divides the periods differently.

driven by the Dutch. The first factory on the *Indian* coast was established at Surat, in 1612, with the consent of the Emperor Jahangir, and this remained their only factory on the West Coast till they obtained Bombay, which had been given to Charles II. as part of the dowry of his Portuguese wife, and was granted to the East India Company by that king in 1668. On the other side of India there was a factory at Hugli (afterwards Calcutta, 1686) on the Ganges, not very far from some factories of the Dutch and French. Quite in the South there were factories at Madras, then called Fort St. George, and at Cuddalur, called Fort St. David. All these factories were chosen for the commercial advantages which they offered as seaports, and as outlets for the trade of the district by which they were surrounded. They were connected with agencies further in the interior, as, for example, at Patna and Benares, but the inland trade was chiefly managed by Indian merchants, who acted as middlemen between the English and the natives. These native agents collected the silk, tea, pepper, and other native products and brought them to the factories, and also helped to distribute the imports which came from England in exchange. The imports were chiefly hardware and bullion. Towards these factories the native powers were, on the whole, very friendly. The small forces which the English maintained at their various stations helped to defend the coast, while the dues and payments on the exports and imports formed in course of time a valuable source of revenue to the native princes.[1]

§ 45. **The Rival East India Company.**—In fact, the native princes were sometimes more friendly than those in power at home. The monopoly which the company

[1] Cf. Carlos, *British India*, p. 34.

possessed had become very unpopular in England. Not only had individual merchants continually tried to infringe its privileges, but rival associations were even formed. Of these the most important was the " New Company," which, though unchartered, strove persistently for freedom of trade. This New Company made two attempts (in 1693 and 1698) to prevent the renewal of the Old Company's charter, but they were foiled by the secret service money which the Old Company freely lavished in Parliament. Nevertheless, Lord Montagu, in the year 1698, established by the help of the Whig party a rival company which was known as the "General East India Company," but it was found after all by the New Company that amalgamation was better than competition, and therefore, after being partially united in 1702, both companies merged into one in 1708 under the title of "The United Company of Merchants of England Trading to the East Indies."

§ 46. **Rivalry of the French Company.**—But even before the close of the period of factories there were signs that the company was likely to become something more than a merely commercial power. The stations of Calcutta, Madras, and Bombay, had developed into presidencies, each of which was ruled by a governor and council of four members appointed by the directors in England. About this period also the company received from Charles II. the important right of making peace and war upon their own account, independently of the home Government. Very soon this power was to be exercised. Although the East India Company had now retreated from its rivalry with the Dutch, and was at peace with them, and although the Portuguese were too weak to give any trouble, a third rival which proved more troublesome than either still remained. This was the "French East India Company," which had been founded in 1624. Their chief factory was at Pondicherry, but they had also other stations on the East Coast, and they possessed in addition the Isle of France (Mauritius) and the Isle of Bourbon, colonies which, though at some distance from India, were afterwards of considerable service as forming a basis of hostile operations against the English. In fact, it was the Governor of Mauritius, Labourdonnais, who was one of the most dangerous enemies of the English company, and it was he who, during the great European War of 1741 to 1748,[1] made preparations for attacking the English factories, and sailed off to Pondicherry to help the governor of the French Presidency there to do so.

§ 47. **Dupleix.**—This governor of the French Presidency on the East Coast of India was Joseph Dupleix, a man who had greatly distinguished himself in the business of the French East India Company in Bengal, and had in return for his services been made governor at Pondicherry. He is famous as being, perhaps, the first European who began the policy of interference with the politics of native states in order thereby to forward the interests of his own nation. It was Dupleix, too, who introduced the system of training native soldiers in European methods. During the hostilities which followed the arrival of Labourdonnais, Madras was captured, and the English were, on more than one occasion, defeated by the French, but at the peace of Aix-la-Chapelle (1748), hostilities were given up and Madras was restored. Nevertheless, it was felt that the

[1] The War of the Austrian Succession, arising between Frederick of Prussia and Maria Theresa of Austria, in which France and England both joined.

struggle was only postponed for a time, and so it proved. It was the policy of the French to encourage dissensions among the rival native powers who were paramount in Southern India, and they had a favourable field for their intrigues. Since the death of the great Mogul—the Emperor Aurungzebe,—in 1708, the empire of the Moguls had been gradually declining; rulers, who were nominally the deputies of the emperor living at Delhi, were at the head of large states, and were practically independent of the sovereign whom they professed to serve. The most important ruler in the South was the Nizam of the Dekkan, with the Nawabs of Mysore and the Karnatic under him; but in addition to these, there were various Marhatta chiefs [1] who were ready to join anyone who would pay for their services, and were constantly causing trouble both in North and South India. Now, it was the policy of Dupleix to win over to the French side the Nawab of the Karnatic who ruled the district in which both the French and English factories stood. However, the Nawab was friendly to the English, but by various intrigues a revolution was effected which placed a prince who was friendly to the French upon the throne. Thereupon the English adopted the cause of a rival, Mahommed Ali, then Governor of Trichinopoli, and, before long, war broke out again, beginning this time with an attack by the Nawab of the Karnatic and the French upon Trichinopoli, which the English forces helped to defend.

[1] The Marhattas were originally Hindu robber clans living in the W. Ghâts around Bombay, who became formidable towards the end of the 17th century, under their leader, Sivaji, and levied systematic blackmail throughout Southern India. Afterwards they became a formidable confederacy of states under a "Peishwa" or chief.

§ 48. **Clive.**—It was at this time that Robert Clive came to the front. To effect a diversion he marched from Madras to Arcot, the Nawab's capital, and captured it, afterwards holding it, when besieged, against a large force. His capture and defence of the town was a turning-point in Anglo-Indian history, for it transferred to the English the prestige which the French had hitherto held as the best European soldiers in India. But the struggle was by no means ended. The defence of Trichinopoli was kept up by Mahommed Ali who finally compelled the French to abandon the siege. Further fighting was still going on when the home Governments, who were at that time at peace, began to interfere, and the result of their inquiries was that Dupleix was removed, and further interference with the native states forbidden. The net result of all these hostilities was that the French had set up a Nizam of the Dekkan favourable to their interests, while the English had made their friend Mahommed Ali the Nawab of the Karnatic.

But almost immediately after the struggle in South India the East India Company had further trouble in the North-East. A new Nawab of Bengal, who had succeeded to the throne in 1756, was unfriendly to the English, and upon some small excuse advanced against and captured Calcutta, and there committed the atrocity which is familiar to all English readers by the name of "the Black Hole of Calcutta." Immediately upon hearing of this, Clive, who was now a Lieutenant-Colonel and Deputy-Governor of Fort St. David, marched with a strong force to Bengal, and advanced up the river Ganges. After destroying the French factories in that district, so as to free himself from any interference on their part, he advanced to Murshedabad, the Nawab's capital, and on June 23, 1757, met the Nawab himself in a fair field in the celebrated battle of Plassey. Here he gained a great victory, and proceeded then to install a friendly ruler, Mir Jafar, as Nawab, though, from the moment that the battle of Plassey was decided, it became clear that not native princes, but English governors, were to be the real rulers of India.

§ 49. **Downfall of French Power in India.**—Still there was much fighting to be done, and in the South the French once more became troublesome. In 1758 a strong expedition of French troops arrived in the Karnatic under the command of Comte de Lally, who immediately captured Fort St. David, and then proceeded to attack Madras. For some time it looked as though the English would be defeated; but in the autumn of the next year Colonel Eyre Coote arrived from England with reinforcements, and then a very severe pitched battle took place at Wandewash (Vandivasu). The battle was fought almost entirely between the French and English troops, for the Sepoys (Sepahis) or natives on either side "stood still in amazement" (to use their own words) at the sight of such a battle as they had never seen before. After heavy fighting, the English were victorious, and Coote now proceeded to reduce all the forts held by the French—finally capturing even their chief station, Pondicherry (January, 1761). This completed the downfall of the French in India, and henceforth whatever troubles we had to meet were only with native princes, and we got through them without the interference of any European power. The English were also supreme in Bengal. Mir Jafar, as a token of his gratitude, gave to Clive the royal revenue of the whole district round Calcutta—known since as Clive's Jagir, which was afterwards transferred to the company for an annuity of £30,000 a year. Clive then returned to England, where he was made a peer in acknowledgment of his services; but he went back to India in 1765. The battle of Buxar, in 1764, when the Emperor of Delhi was defeated, finally confirmed English authority in the North-East. Yet it must be remembered that the conquest of India was accomplished to a large extent by native soldiers who were trained under our own system of military discipline. During all the period of which we have been speaking, the English contingent in the East India Company's army was never more, and often less, than one-fifth of the whole, the remaining four-fifths being Sepoys.

CHAPTER XI.

THE CONQUEST OF INDIA, A.D. 1761-1857.

§ 50. **Clive's Reforms: North's Regulating Act.**—Having now gained a commanding position both in Northern and Southern India, Clive next proceeded to place political affairs upon a sounder basis, and to reform certain abuses which prevailed. It was arranged with the Emperor, in consideration of certain payments from the company, that he should recognise their possession of Bengal, Behar, and Orissa, so that the company was now practically in the same position as that formerly held by the Nawabs of Bengal. Then Clive stopped private[1] trading and replaced it by a monopoly of salt, tobacco, and betel, which was managed by the company. He also established military stations in various places for the defence of the country, and, generally speaking, restored order and administration where confusion and corruption had previously prevailed. We must attribute to Clive the establishment of British rule in India upon a firm footing. The work of his successors was to develop and expand what he had begun. Clive finally left India in 1767, and nothing further of importance occurred till the appointment of Warren Hastings as Governor of

[1] *i.e.* Trade carried on by factors and clerks of the East India Company for their own profit.

Bengal in 1772. Shortly before his appointment an awful famine had occurred in Bengal (1770), whereby, it is said, that a third of the population perished. By this calamity the officials of the company, to their lasting shame, enriched themselves; but in 1773 the finances of the company itself were in such a desperate state that the home Government had to relieve them by a loan. At the same time Lord North's Act for the Regulation of India was passed, commonly called "The Regulating Act" (1773). It established a supreme court of justice whose judges were appointed by the Crown. The Governor of Bengal was made Governor-General of India, and a council of five was appointed to help the governor. But although this Act shows a certain amount of interference on the part of the home Government, the directors of the company were still allowed to elect the governor-general.

§ 51. **Warren Hastings.**—Under Warren Hastings the company's dominion was greatly extended, and the finances of the company were placed on a sound basis. The collection of the revenue was placed under European officers, although in order to provide for the immediate necessaries of the company, Hastings exacted large sums from native chiefs, and also introduced the system of requiring native states who were in subjection to the company to support a portion of the English forces in India. As everybody knows, his administration was subjected to severe criticism, and he himself had to stand a long and weary trial of seven years. But although we may admit that he committed some faults, it should, nevertheless, be remembered that during his administration (1772 to 1785), when we were engaged in the War of American Independence, and a very harassing war with France, he succeeded in preserving peace

THE CONQUEST OF INDIA, A.D. 1761-1857. 75

in British India for England, without asking the mother country for any help. This is the more remarkable because Hastings had to encounter formidable enemies amongst native princes. Hyder Ali invaded the Karnatic (1780), but was repulsed, and the triple alliance of Ali, the Nizam, and the Marhattas was also defeated, though his son, Tippu, continued to give trouble on the Malabar coast.

§ 52. **Fox's and Pitt's Bills.**—During Warren Hastings' administration, another political arrangement was proposed for the Government of India, which is known as Fox's India Bill (1783), by which the authority of the company was transferred to seven commissioners nominated by Parliament, and, when vacancies occurred, by the Crown, while the management of the property and the commerce of the company was entrusted to a subordinate council of directors nominated by the court of proprietors. This bill, though passed by the Commons, was rejected by the Lords at the instigation of George III., but was followed next year by Pitt's India Bill. This second bill, which duly passed, established a Board of Control, consisting of six members of the Privy Council, including one Secretary of State and the Chancellor of the Exchequer, with supreme authority over the administration of the company both in civil and military affairs. Commerce, business, and patronage were still left in the hands of the company, but the Crown was to have the right of a veto in the case of appointment to the chief offices. This board lasted till after the Mutiny, and was only dissolved in 1858. Thus the political and commercial affairs of the company became separated, the former being now very largely under the direct influence of the home Government.

§ 53. **Further History to 1818.**—We have now only space left to go very briefly into the history of the further development of India. Warren Hastings was succeeded in 1786 by Lord Cornwallis (1786 to 1793), who reformed the company's civil service, and introduced the permanent settlement of the land revenue of Bengal, which was based on the payments made from the land in the previous years. By this settlement the Zemindars, who collected the revenue from the villages, became practically landlords of the districts under them, on condition of paying a fixed rent to the Government. This settlement, however, applied only to Bengal, different systems being introduced later in Madras, Bombay, and the North-West Provinces. During Lord Cornwallis' administration, the policy of non-intervention was pursued towards the native states, but under the Marquis of Wellesley (1798 to 1805) the dominion of the British in India was greatly extended. He engaged in war with Tippu Sultan (whose father, Ali, had seized Mysore, and who himself was very hostile to the British), and crushed his power in the fourth Mysore war which ended in the capture of Seringapatam in 1799. The Marhatta confederacy was then broken up by the treaty of Bassein (1802), and though other Marhatta wars followed, in which Sir Arthur Wellesley (afterwards the Duke of Wellington) took part, the power of the Marhatta states was greatly curtailed, and the political influence of the company, as well as its dominions, was largely increased. The power of the company continued to progress under subsequent governors, and was again increased in 1818 by the annexation of the territory of the Peishwa,[1] which was annexed to the Bombay Presidency. And now the dominion of the

[1] The chief of the Marhatta Confederacy of States. The Peishwas were originally only hereditary ministers of the ruling house, but had usurped the power of their masters.

THE CONQUEST OF INDIA, A.D. 1761-1857. 77

company began to extend beyond the limits of India itself, for under the governorship of Lord Amherst occurred the first Burmese war, which was caused by the encroachments of the King of Ava upon British territory, and resulted in our gaining the provinces of Aracan, Tenasserim, and to a certain extent Assam.

§ 54. **Abolition of the Company.**—But the power of the company was now being merged into the power of England itself, and its actions were in reality the actions of the British Government. Its commercial privileges also now became seriously affected. In 1813 its monopoly of trade with India was abolished, and though it was allowed to keep its monopoly with China, it was forced to allow Europeans to trade with India quite freely. Twenty years later (1833) the charter of the company was renewed, but only on condition that it altogether abandoned its trading, even including the Chinese monopoly. Its commercial property was sold, and it became distinctly a political body, but its dominion over India was confirmed for only twenty years. Soon after these twenty years had elapsed, the company received its death-blow from the Indian Mutiny of 1857. It had long been seen that it stood in quite an anomalous position, and the Mutiny only precipitated a change of Government which was sure to come sooner or later. In 1858 was passed the "Act for the better government of India," which provided that the entire administration of the country should be transferred to the Crown. The Crown was to govern through a "Secretary of State for India," who was assisted by a council of fifteen, while the governor-general was henceforth to be called Viceroy. At the same time the naval and military forces of the company were united with those of the Crown.

§ 55. **Development of India.**—By thus referring to the death of the old company we have anticipated the order of events in the development of India, and we may now shortly refer to them. Under the governorship of Lord William Bentinck (1828 to 1835) steam navigation to India was first introduced, and various educational and judicial measures of great value were passed. Then came the first Afghan War (1839 to 1842) and the conquest of Sind by Sir Charles Napier. The first Sikh War ended in 1846, though it was not till the end of the second Sikh War that the Sikhs submitted. Their country was annexed, and shortly afterwards the second Burmese War gave us further possessions on the sea-coast of Burmah. These two last wars took place under the administration of Lord Dalhousie (1848 to 1856), whose policy of annexation, though much criticised at the time, has proved, on the whole, very beneficial both to the conqueror and the conquered. Lord Dalhousie also did much for the general development of the resources of the country by promoting the introduction of railways and telegraphs, the making of good roads, and the establishment of irrigation works. But just as everything seemed going on smoothly and the country seemed to be developing its resources in a peaceful manner, the great Mutiny broke out, and for a short time it seemed as if the whole fabric of British rule would be utterly demolished. As all know, it was saved by the bravery of our troops, and since then, in spite of occasional difficulties, chiefly with the tribes on the frontier, and with the Afghans, peace has prevailed and prosperity has spread over the country. In 1877 the Queen assumed the title of Empress of India, thus restoring a dignity which had been in abeyance since the deposition of the last titular emperor in 1857.

§ 56. **Review of the Company's Progress.** — With this we may conclude our sketch of the growth of the British power in India, and of the progress and abolition of the ancient East India Company. It may be well, however, to remember that although this company was politically of such importance, it was hardly ever quite so flourishing commercially as has been commonly supposed. The influence of the monopoly which it possessed seemed, like all monopolies, to have deadened, or, at any rate, to have checked in a large degree the natural progress of trade and industry. In 1780, for instance, the East India trade only formed one thirty-second part of the total foreign trade of the United Kingdom, and up to the present century the exports from India had never averaged more than a million a year. Soon after the abolition of the monopoly they began to rise, till in 1834 they amounted to £10,000,000, and in the next fifty years were increased more than sixfold, being worth £66,000,000 in 1880, and £70,000,000 in 1890. Thus, since the monopoly was abolished, our trade with India began to assume those proportions which we should naturally have expected in the case of so rich a country. But in the old days, when corruption and maladministration were rife, while the servants of the company frequently returned home with large fortunes, the general finances and trade of the company itself were not at all satisfactory. Nevertheless, if its commercial enterprise is open to criticism, we should remember that, after all, trade and commerce are not everything, and that the political services of the company in gaining for us an empire of almost infinite wealth, are not to be lightly esteemed.

We may notice that in recent years a great development has taken place in regard to the trade in tea and wheat exported from India, and that these two commodities have done much to increase the riches of the country. More tea is now exported from India to England than comes to us from China, whereas at one time we used to use Chinese tea almost exclusively. Large areas, especially in the North-West of India, are also now under wheat, which has become a very valuable crop to Indian growers. It should also be remembered that India, especially since the opening of the Suez Canal (p. 107), holds a very important commercial position as the great intermediary for commerce between England and the East generally, being, on a large scale, an emporium such as Hong Kong and Singapore are as single ports (p. 126.)

CHAPTER XII.

THE AMERICAN COLONIES AND THEIR SEPARATION.

§ 57. **Trade with America.**—We have seen in a previous chapter how our colonies in America were founded, and how they began to develop. We have seen that they grew with great rapidity considering the difficulties which they had to face, for the population, which numbered 200,000 in 1688, had risen to 375,750 in 1714, and was at least a million and a half in 1756. A considerable commerce was also growing up between North America and England; the exports being chiefly tobacco, rice, grain, hides, skins, furs, and fish, while in return English merchants sent cloth, furniture, hardware, and other manufactured articles. Our colonial trade, however, was hampered by the system of monopoly, which, as we have seen, dominated all the commercial dealings of the 17th and 18th centuries; and soon this theory was to prove in practice a fatal mistake. Let us, therefore, look rather more closely at the commercial relations which existed at this time between the colonies and the mother country.

§ 58. **Commercial Policy of England.**—It has been frequently said that the establishment of our American and West Indian colonies was a device of the supporters of the Mercantile System, who founded them in the view of raising a population, chiefly agricultural in character, whose commerce should be confined entirely to an exchange of their raw products for our manufactured goods.[1] This, however, is not entirely true. There is not the least doubt that at first the colonists were allowed to carry on a direct intercourse with foreign states, and, in fact, their charters empowered them to do so. The Virginian settlers, for example, established tobacco warehouses in Middleburgh and Flushing in 1620, as depôts for their trade with the Continent. It was not till the time of the Navigation Acts (1651 and 1660), that the import and export trade of the colonies was actually monopolised by their mother country. The first of these Acts, as we know, enacted that the trade of the colonists should be carried on exclusively in British or colonial ships, but the second Act (that of 12 Charles II., c. 18) went much further than this, for it enacted that certain specified articles—in fact, the chief products of the colonies—should not be exported directly from the colonies to any foreign country, but must be first sent to Britain, and there, in the words of the Act, "unladen, and laid upon the shore," before they could be forwarded to their ultimate destination, if they were meant for any European market. These articles became known by the name of "enumerated articles," and were originally limited to sugar, molasses, ginger, fustic, tobacco, cotton, and indigo; but afterwards coffee, hides, iron, corn, and lumber were added. Moreover, not content with making the colonists sell their goods only in the English markets, it was enacted further that no goods should be imported into the British colonies unless they were actually first laden and put on board at some British port,[2] so that all commercial intercourse, both of export and

[1] Cf. McCulloch's *Commercial Dictionary* ("Colonies"). The whole article on "Colonies" is worth careful reading.

[2] The restrictions above mentioned were frequently evaded.

THE AMERICAN COLONIES. 83

import trade, had to go first through British hands. Further still, manufactures in the colonies themselves were also discouraged, and so far was this principle carried, that Lord Chatham did not hesitate to declare in Parliament that "the British colonists of North America had no right to manufacture even a nail for a horse-shoe." With aggravating restrictions of this character, it was almost certain that sooner or later ill-feeling would arise among the colonists; and, as a matter of fact, long before the War of Independence, this ill-feeling was gaining ground; so that the special circumstances that led to the war were only the secondary causes of a movement which was from the nature of the case inevitable.

Before, however, we come to the struggle for independence, we must give a short glance at the position and extent of our colonies at the beginning and middle of the 18th century.

§ 59. **Position and Growth of the American Colonies.**—They were localised, as we have seen, in three groups, and now extended from the river Kennebec to Florida. On the north, that which is now the Canadian Dominion was then entirely in the hands of the French, whose colonies extended down the basin of the Mississippi; for French explorers, having discovered the source of this great river, traced its course down to the sea in 1682, and claimed all the lands on its banks, naming them Louisiana[1] in honour of King Louis XIV. Thus the English were shut in both on the north and west, being confined to that portion of land which lies between the Alleghany Mountains

[1] It will be seen that what is now called Louisiana is only a very small portion of a territory which once extended from the mouth of the Mississippi to the great lakes.

and the Atlantic Ocean, while their boundary on the south was the Spanish colony of Florida. Hence, though the English in America numbered over 1,500,000 colonists to the 60,000 colonists of France, the latter, from a military point of view, had certainly the best of the position. During the wars which went on in Europe between William III. and Louis XIV., the French and English colonists in America maintained a good deal of desultory fighting, but when the European War terminated, England secured great advantages in North America by the Treaty of Utrecht in 1713. This treaty gave to her Newfoundland, the Hudson Bay territory (originally occupied by the French), Nova Scotia, and New Brunswick. Canada proper, however, was not yet ours. The position of affairs remained very much as before till about 1754, when an English company attempted to colonise a territory on the banks of the Ohio.

§ 60. **Conquest of Canada.**—Now the French had claims on all lands lying west of the Alleghany Mountains, and had just built a fort there, called Fort Duquesne, in order to protect their claim. Consequently a conflict between the French and English settlers occurred. A young man named George Washington, who was then quite unknown to history, attempted to drive the French out, but failed in the attempt. Meanwhile the French lost no time in improving their military position, and Montcalm, the French governor of Canada, thought it a favourable opportunity to link together the three chief French forts in that region (namely, Duquesne, Niagara, and Ticonderoga) by a series of smaller forts, which would thus give him a very strong frontier. It was at this point that the English Government at home thought the matter sufficiently serious to interfere, and therefore sent out a body of troops under

THE AMERICAN COLONIES. 85

General Braddock. This general was defeated and slain in 1755, but in the next year, when the Seven Years' War broke out in Europe, the home Government, at the suggestion of Pitt, sent out reinforcements to America, and assisted the English colonists to attack Quebec and Montreal (then the chief French towns in Canada). Thereupon the war between the colonists was actively continued, and, as is well known, the English succeeded in gaining possession of these towns. When peace was made in Europe by the Treaty of Paris in 1763, England gained all the French possessions in North America except Louisiana, and the colonies were allowed to extend as far as they might wish. So complete was the ruin of the French power, that in despair of making any use of a territory which was now completely isolated, France gave up Louisiana to her friend and neighbour Spain.

§ 61. **Attempts to raise a Revenue from America.—** Circumstances had therefore now become very favourable for the building up in America of a colonial empire as rich as that of India, but whose population, unlike that of the last, should consist almost entirely of English settlers. This pleasant vision, however, was never to be realised. The time of separation was approaching. It probably would have come in any case owing to the mistaken policy of the home Government in regard to colonial trade, but the immediate cause was the attempt made to raise a revenue from the colonies without first gaining their assent thereto, and without allowing them representation at home. The revenue was needed in order to pay for the expenses of the Seven Years' War, in which conflict it cannot be denied that the colonists had received substantial help from their mother country, and had gained substantial benefits. Therefore it did not seem unfair that they should be asked to contribute towards lightening a burden, which had to some extent been incurred on their behalf. And indeed the request in itself was not altogether unreasonable, but the colonists resented the manner in which it was made, and refused to assent to the principle of taxation without representation. The history of the struggle that followed is too well known to need further repetition. It began with the Stamp Act of 1765, which laid a tax upon the stamps required for legal purposes. This succeeded in irritating the colonists to such an extent that they refused to have any commercial intercourse with the mother country, and so powerful was their opposition that it produced a considerable decline in the colonial trade with England, and English manufacturers themselves requested that the Act might be repealed. This was done in 1776, but the next year the "six duties"[1] were imposed on the ground that it was "expedient that a revenue should be raised in His Majesty's dominions in America." But the opposition of the colonists was so great that it was found impossible to collect the duties, and they were therefore all repealed except that on tea, though a preamble to the Act regarding the tea duty still asserted the right of the home Government to tax its colonies.

§ 62. **Outbreak of War.**—Then came the refusal of the citizens of Boston to pay even this tax, and their well-known feat of throwing a cargo of tea, from the ship that brought it, into their harbour (1773). Lord North, the chief minister of George III. at that time, tried to punish

[1] So called because they were imposed upon six articles, including glass, tea, paper, red and white lead, painters' colours and pasteboard. They were estimated to produce about £40,000 for the purpose of paying colonial judges and governors.

the Bostonians by declaring their port closed, and by annulling the charter of Massachusetts, their colony. Thus matters went from bad to worse, until, in 1775, all trade with the colonies was forbidden, and the rupture with the mother country was completed by the Declaration of Independence on July 4th, 1776. England tried to enforce obedience by military power, but the royal troops were stoutly resisted, and though the fortunes of war frequently varied, and the colonists were often defeated, the result was that they achieved their independence. It should be noted that Spain and France took the opportunity of paying off their ancient grudge against England by helping her colonists against her, chiefly by means of their navies. And it should also be noticed that, in spite of every difficulty, England only just failed to retain her hold upon the colonies, and that if the French had not interfered, it is very possible that the colonists would never have succeeded in becoming independent, at any rate not till many years later than they actually did. As it was, however, we lost the opportunity of founding a really great colonial empire, and alienated the sympathies of a large number of our fellow-countrymen. Nevertheless, as has been pointed out,[1] there were great compensations for our loss. As the new nation prospered, our trade with it increased; and as American agriculture developed, the demand for our manufactures in the United States market became greater also; while in the East we were at this time obtaining several new markets hitherto monopolised by Holland. Certainly, from a commercial point of view, the war did our trade very little harm, for soon after it ended we notice a considerable increase in the imports and exports to and from the colonies.[2]

[1] Caldecott, *English Colonisation and Empire*, p. 57.
[2] Cf. Craik, *Hist. Brit. Comm.*, iii. 102.

CHAPTER XIII.

THE INDUSTRIAL REVOLUTION AND THE CONTINENTAL WAR.

§ 63. **The Old Conditions of Industry.**—We have now come to the period to which has been given the very appropriate name of the Industrial Revolution, a period in which the most important changes took place, not only in our economic life, but in politics and society as well. With political and social questions we have not here to deal, but the industrial changes have been so remarkable that they deserve our most careful consideration.

The beginning of the Industrial Revolution is usually placed between 1750 and 1770. Before that time the use of machinery had been very limited, and steam power, now the greatest motive force in common use, was never employed at all. Manufactures were carried on under what was known as the "Domestic System;" that is, not in large factories where numbers of people are gathered together, all working at the same time and with the same machinery, but in people's own homes, in the domestic circle, where the father and mother were aided by their children and apprentices. Then again there were no railways or canals, so that the means of communication were comparatively few, and were rendered still more difficult by the bad state into which the roads had fallen in the 18th century. Again, the

THE INDUSTRIAL REVOLUTION. 89

methods of mining were very imperfect, so that even if the modern machinery had been invented, it would have been almost impossible to get sufficient motive power to work it. But all these old conditions of industry were in a very few years completely changed, and the whole industrial system was transformed. The first impulse came from a series of inventions that occurred very rapidly one after the other.

§ 64. **The Great Inventions.**—The first of these was the steam-engine of James Watt, who took out his patent in the year 1769, though it was not applied to manufacturing processes until some years later, being first used only in mining operations. It was the inventions of machinery, and not of steam-engines to work them, that were first used. In 1770, James Hargreaves patented the "spinning-jenny," that is, a frame with a number of spindles side by side which were fed by machinery and by which many threads might be fed at once instead of only one, as had been the case in the old spinning-wheel. The next year another well-known inventor, named Arkwright, set up a successful mill in which was employed the "water-frame," an invention which derived its name from the fact that it was worked by water power. Not many years later (1779) Crompton invented the "mule," which was so called because it combined the peculiarities of both the previous inventions. It drew out the roving (that is, the raw material when it has received its first twist) by an adaptation of the water-frame, and then passed it on to be finished and twisted into complete yarn by another adaptation of the "spinning-jenny." This invention at once caused an enormous increase in production, and at the present time, since it has been perfected, 12,000 spindles are often worked by it at once, and by one spinner. It was from the very first so successful, that by the year 1811 more than four and a half million spindles worked by "mules" were being employed in various English factories. These three inventions, however, only increased the power of spinning; what was now wanted was an invention that would increase the power of weaving into cloth the threads thus spun. Before long the required invention was discovered by Cartwright, and was patented in 1785 under the name of the "power loom" though it was not employed to a very large extent until 1813. But the year of its invention is noticeable as being also the year in which James Watt's steam-engine was first introduced into factories, and, of course, as soon as it was introduced the enormous advantage of steam over water was at once felt. An instance of the tremendous changes it caused may be seen in the cotton trade, which was the first to employ steam power on a large scale, and which in the fourteen years from 1788 to 1802 was trebled in volume.[1]

§ 65. **Mining and Canals.**—It will be easily perceived that the new development in manufacturing textile goods necessitated a corresponding development in the production of coal and iron, because the newly invented machinery required large quantities of iron to make it, and still larger quantities of coal to work it. Hitherto coal had hardly been worked in any large quantities, because there was no adequate means of pumping water out of the mines until steam power could be used for that purpose. But now, as the mines could be better worked, both coal and iron were produced in large quantities, and the immense mineral wealth which

[1] In 1788 over 20,000,000 lbs. of cotton were imported for manufacture; and in 1802 just over 60,000,000 lbs. See McCulloch's *Dictionary*, art. "Cotton."

lies beneath the surface of English soil began for the first time to be properly developed. Whilst these great inventions and developments were going on in mining and the production of merchandise, equally important steps were being taken to facilitate the distribution thereof. The first and most noticeable of these was the making of canals; the first canal being cut from the Duke of Bridgewater's colliery at Worsley to the neighbouring town of Manchester (1761). The Bridgewater canal was followed by a large number of other waterways throughout the whole country, and the rivers of England, which had always been used to some considerable extent for commercial purposes, were now connected one with another; so that, with canals and rivers together, there was a complete network of communication by water all over the country. Roads were also greatly improved, and though railways were not invented until some time later, it will be seen that the facilities for communication were thus considerably promoted.

§ 66. **Political Circumstances of the Times.**—We have thus seen that the Industrial Revolution procured for English merchants and manufacturers the means of producing large quantities of merchandise, and it so happened that, from the political circumstances of the time, England gained an almost unrivalled position for disposing of her goods in foreign markets. If we look at the state of the European powers after the conclusion of the Seven Years' War in 1763, we shall see how favourable our position then was. In the first place, England had seriously crippled her commercial rival, France, both in her Indian and American possessions, and thereby had gained extensive colonial territories which afforded a ready market for British goods. Spain, which had been allied with France, had lost at the same time her position as the commercial rival of England in trade with the New World. Germany had for some time ceased to be a formidable competitor, and was now being ravaged by internal conflicts between the reigning houses of Austria and Prussia. Holland, which had once been England's most serious rival—especially in foreign commerce—was at this time in a similar condition, and had greatly declined from the prosperity of the 16th and 17th centuries. Hence England alone had the chance of "the universal empire of the sole market." The supply of this market was in the hands of English manufacturers and English workmen, so that the great inventions which came into operation after 1763 were thus at once called into active employment, and our mills and mines were able to produce wealth as fast as they could work, without fear of foreign competition.

§ 67. **Growth of Foreign Trade: The French War.**—It is not surprising, therefore, to find that in the ten years, from 1782 to 1792, our entire foreign trade was nearly doubled, the exact figures being:—

1782	Imports £10,341,628	Exports £13,009,458
1792	,, £19,659,358	,, £24,905,200

And this remarkable progress was still kept up even during the great continental wars which were caused by the French Revolution, and which lasted for almost a quarter of a century. Indeed, it is very remarkable how steadily our home industries and our foreign trade progressed in spite of the great political and financial dangers to which this period of war exposed us.

THE INDUSTRIAL REVOLUTION. 93

Of course we have not space here to go into the various causes which led to war with France; it is sufficient to state that war was formally declared on the 1st February, 1793, and as the result of the unsettled condition of European politics at that time, there was a severe commercial crisis in England, marked by a large number of bankruptcies, and the stoppage of nearly one-third of the provincial banks. The next effect of the war was to destroy entirely the trade with France, which had sprung up since the Eden Treaty of 1786.[1] Our trade with Holland was also much injured, because that country was invaded by the French, and was compelled to refuse admittance to English goods. Then, in 1795, France concluded an alliance with Prussia and Spain, and thus our trade with these countries also almost ceased. Most of the Italian princes or dukes were also allied to France, and thus in a very short time nearly all the ports of Southern Europe, except those of Portugal, Turkey, and our own Gibraltar, were shut against our manufactures.

[1] This treaty was negotiated by William Eden, afterwards Lord Auckland, and should be noticed as a relaxation of the almost traditional policy of commercial enmity with France, of which the Methuen Treaty was an example. In the three years before the treaty was made, our exports to France had not averaged half a million sterling in value, but from 1786 to 1793 they averaged more than a million per annum.

CHAPTER XIV.

ENGLAND DURING THE WAR—THE UNION WITH IRELAND.

§ 68. **Effect of the War.**—Strange though it may seem, however, in spite of the almost entire loss of our trade in some directions, English commerce improved in others; and, in fact, any loss was more than counterbalanced by an increase in regard to the (now independent) United States, Russia, Venice, Germany, and Northern Europe, as well as with the West and East Indian colonies, both British and foreign. In fact, many of the countries whom France had compelled to become our enemies found themselves unable to do without British manufactures, especially as their own industries were suffering from the warfare that was going on on the Continent, and therefore had to find means to procure our goods.

§ 69. **Napoleon's Decrees.**—But Napoleon, who probably suspected this, now proceeded to adopt still more stringent means for crushing English commerce. By the celebrated Berlin Decree of the 21st November, 1806, he ordered (1) that the British Islands should be declared in a state of blockade; (2) that all correspondence and letters with them should be prohibited; (3) that any British subjects found in any country occupied by the French, or their allies, should be at once taken prisoner; (4) that all goods and merchandise belonging to British subjects should be a lawful prize of war; (5) that all commerce in British commodities should be prohibited; and (6) that no vessel coming from England or her colonies should be allowed to enter any French port, or any port subject to French authority. To this comprehensive measure the English Government replied by the Orders in Council of the 7th January and the 11th February, 1807, which were of much the same character as Napoleon's decree, and also warned neutral ships not to trade with French or allied ports.[1] Then Napoleon issued another famous decree, this time from Milan, on the 17th December, 1807, which was the exact opposite of the English Orders, and decreed that all British goods found in France, Germany, Holland, Italy, or any other place occupied by French troops, should be seized and burned. This sort of thing, however, did very little harm to English commerce, since fresh goods were required to take the place of those that had been so recklessly destroyed.

§ 70. **Colonies and Trade during the War.**—On the whole, then, the war was not very disastrous to us; and we gained during its progress some very considerable additions to our colonial possessions. In 1793 and subsequent years we gained from the French many of their settlements in the West Indies, including Trinidad and Tobago. From the Dutch we captured Malacca, Ceylon (1796), Demerara (1803), and the Cape of Good Hope

---

[1] The question of the right of neutral ships to trade with powers who were at war, and also of the right of those powers to search them, was frequently productive of much unpleasantness between England and other nations, as, for example, in the case of the Armed Neutralities of 1780 and 1800. The question of the right of search caused another war between England and the United States in 1812.

(1806).[1] At the same time, as we have seen elsewhere, we made important extensions of our power in India, and also developed an entirely new field of colonial enterprise in Australia by the establishment in 1788 of a convict settlement in Botany Bay, which afterwards became New South Wales. (See p. 121). Even our exports increased during the war, as the following table will show:—

Year.	Imports.	Exports.	Total.
1790	£16,398,000	£17,636,000	£34,034,000
1800	28,258,000	34,382,000	62,640,000
1810	39,302,000	48,439,000	87,741,000

A new market of considerable extent was also opened for us in South America, partly from the fact that the Portuguese Government was compelled to transfer itself bodily from Lisbon to Brazil in 1808, and partly because most of the Spanish colonists there became practically emancipated from their mother country about this time. It should also be remembered that we had a great advantage over every other country in the fact that our navy was at that time so successful in meeting every opponent, and thus preserved for our almost exclusive use the great ocean highways.

§ 71. **Financial Difficulties: Suspension of Cash Pay-**

[1] "The two points at which British ambition aimed were the security of the sea route to India and the extension of the production of sugar in the West Indies. The first design was satisfied by the occupation of the Cape of Good Hope; the second by the capture of Guiana and of some of the West Indian Islands hitherto held by the French." Gardiner, *Student's History*, p. 858.

ments.—But before concluding this hasty sketch of the great period of the Continental War, we ought to mention the financial difficulties into which, in spite of commercial prosperity, it plunged our country. None but a rich State could ever have stood the terrible effects of this war so well as England bore them at this time;[1] but even as it was, the strain was tremendous. The war actually cost from first to last no less than £831,446,449, and more than £600,000,000 were added to the National Debt.[2] William Pitt, who was then Prime Minister, tried every means of raising money, not only by increasing duties on almost every article that could be taxed, but also by a system of loans. The duties were placed upon spirits, plate, brick, stones, glass, wine, tea, coffee, fruit, hats, horses, and dogs; and these were followed by a heavy income tax, till very soon there were very few articles of any description that were left untaxed. Loans had also been raised by the Government upon a system which has since proved very disadvantageous to the country at large, because such easy terms were given to the lenders that practically very little more than 75 per cent. was received for every £100 nominally subscribed. Thus between 1793 and 1801 no

---

[1] "Pitt's main support lay in the extraordinary financial resources supplied by the rapidly increasing manufactures of England." S. R. Gardiner, *History of England*, p. 835.

[2] At this period (1793) the revenue from taxation only was £19,845,705, and the expenditure £24,197,070. In 1815 the revenue was £72,210,512, and the expenditure £92,280,180. At the beginning of the war with Russia in 1855, the National Debt was £805,411,690; in 1882 it had been reduced to £754,455,270; and in 1890 to £689,944,027, the annual interest and annuities on which amount to some £25,000,000. Cf. W. Hewins' article in the *Co-operative Annual*, 1889.

less than eighteen different loans were raised by Pitt, but for the nominal capital of £314,000,000 that were funded as National Debt, only £202,000,000, or only 65 per cent., were really received in cash. Heavy subsidies were also given to our continental allies, chiefly Prussia and Austria. No less than £4,000,000 were sent to Austria in 1796. The awful strain upon the resources of the country naturally led to a severe commercial crisis, and even the Bank of England was directed to suspend cash payments of its notes (26th February, 1797). These notes, which now could not be turned into cash, were nevertheless accepted loyally by all the principal merchants, and, following their example, by all classes of the community; and for more than twenty years the bank was not permitted to cash its own notes. Such was the crisis through which the commerce of the country had to pass, and that it passed through it successfully says much for English energy and perseverance. But if it had not been that the Industrial Revolution—and the inventions which caused it—had come, as it were, just in time to increase our national wealth, it is very doubtful whether the nation could have passed so successfully through an ordeal so severe as this.

§ 72. **Union with Ireland: Irish Commerce.**—In this terrible period of conflict, however, occurred a peaceful event which, at least from the commercial side, tended to produce better relations between England and her Irish subjects, namely, the Act of Union that was brought about by William Pitt, by which Act many restrictions upon Irish trade were removed, and greater commercial freedom was established between the two countries.[1] To perceive fully the reform herein made, we must glance briefly at the history

[1] Trade restrictions were not fully removed till 1825.

of Irish commerce in the last two centuries. At the death of Elizabeth, Ireland, after much resistance, had become a conquered country. James I. tried to make the conquest more secure by the "Plantation of Ulster," *i.e.*, by giving English or Scotch settlers land in Ulster, as was done on later occasions also in Leitrim, Wicklow, Wexford, and other counties—and Cromwell proceeded, only with greater severity, upon a similar plan. A development of material prosperity might have reconciled the Irish to these proceedings in course of time, but this development was rendered difficult [1] by the regulations affecting their external trade. The only time when prosperity seemed likely to shine upon "the distressful country," was under the rule of Wentworth, Earl of Strafford, whom Charles I. sent out as Deputy-Lord. Strafford suppressed piracy, encouraged commerce, and established manufactures, chief among them the linen trade, which has flourished to this day. [2] He secured for Ireland the victualling of the Spanish fleets for America, reduced the duties which had been placed upon Irish exports; and, in fact, by his magnificent policy of "thorough," restored good order, peace and prosperity, where all had been chaos and misery before. Unfortunately, Strafford's policy was not followed up; on the contrary, Irish trade was crushed by the jealousy of English merchants. Ireland was excluded from the Navigation Acts, and thus was placed upon the footing of a foreign country. Acts of 1665 and

[1] At the same time there was nothing in the nature of these regulations to prevent the internal prosperity of Ireland from reaching a higher point than its people have hitherto been able to attain.

[2] He (no doubt conscientiously) discouraged, on the other hand, such trades as might compete with English trade; *e.g.*, the woollen manufacture. (Knowles, *Strafford Letters*, i. 193.) For his work, cf. Cunningham, ii. 135-137.

1680 prevented the importation of Irish cattle, butter, cheese, and other provisions into England lest they should compete with the produce of the English landowner. The colonial trade was ruined in 1696; and, just as steady progress was being made with the woollen manufacture, the English Parliament in 1699 forbade the export of woollen goods from Ireland to any country except to England, where prohibitive import duties already practically shut them out. It is to the credit of Pitt, that, nearly a century later (1785), he made a proposal for commercial union between England and Ireland, under which there was to be complete free trade between the two countries.[1] But the English manufacturers raised such an outcry at this that Pitt was compelled to re-introduce into his scheme several restrictions on Irish commerce, whereupon the Dublin Parliament rejected the plan altogether. Fortunately, however, Pitt was more successful in after years, and by the Act of Union, which took effect on 1st January, 1801, restrictions upon Irish trade were very largely removed. Since then some progress has been made. Twenty years ago the principal exports were cattle, corn, and other products of agriculture and the dairy; also linen, yarn, and flax, and copper and lead ore.[2] But now both corn and flax are imported, and though the linen trade is still very important, especially in Ulster, most of the flax comes from Belgium; while the area under wheat is very small and rapidly diminishing.[3] Pigs, bacon,

[1] Lord North also had attempted in 1779 to remove the chief commercial disabilities of Ireland, and a serious effort was made to stimulate Irish agriculture and industry—cf. Cunningham (ii. 526), who is very careful and thorough in all the sections dealing with Ireland.
[2] Sullivan's Geography, Dublin, 1874.
[3] Prof. C. F. Bastable.

butter, and cattle are exported still, and also stout and whisky; but the tabinet industry of Dublin, once fairly important, is now decaying, and the Limerick lace trade of former times is quite extinct.[1]

[1] Prof. C. F. Bastable.

CHAPTER XV.

COMMERCE SINCE 1815—THE ERA OF FREE TRADE.

§ 73. **Figures of Trade in 1820.**—The close of the 25 years of continental war (1815) is sometimes taken as being the date when the modern system of commerce may be said to have had its beginning. Up to that time, although great changes and advances had been made, the spirit of monopoly and the general restrictive policy which characterised previous centuries, were still, to some extent, in force. But not very long after the peace that was won by the battle of Waterloo, a remarkable change was made in the commercial policy of England, and the example thus set was followed to some extent—though in a much smaller degree—by other countries. That is to say, we now come to the beginnings of freedom of trade. Free trade did not come all at once, though it came rapidly, for it took fully a quarter of a century before England finally adopted it as a policy and repealed the Corn Laws. The year 1820 may be taken as the first public beginning of the "free trade" movement, and this year also may be specially noticed, because we can gain from a study of it a very good idea of the trade of the country soon after the war, and just before "free trade" measures were begun. In this year the official value of foreign and colonial imports was declared at some £32,000,000, which, with a population of about

THE ERA OF FREE TRADE. 103

19,000,000, was at the rate of 33s. per head.[1] The exports of home produce amounted to some £36,000,000, while the tonnage of shipping entering and leaving our harbours was 4,000,000 tons; of which considerably more than one half belonged to the United Kingdom and its dependencies; though steamers were, of course, as yet unknown. That great authority, Professor Leone Levi, calculates that the trade of the country about this period was no more than one-eighth or one-ninth of what it is at the present time, and that the wealth and comfort obtainable by the nation as a whole was much more limited. In fact, if we compare the huge figures of recent years with those of 1820, we see at once how gigantic has been the growth of our trade. In 1820 the imports and exports *combined* only amount to £79,300,000, or about £4 per head of population, whereas in 1890 they reached £749,000,000, or £20 per head. During the same period the commercial intercourse between Great Britain and her colonies has been almost entirely created.

§ 74. **Free Trade Movement: Huskisson's Reforms.**—That our trade has increased so rapidly, is, without doubt, due in a large measure to the more enlightened policy which Englishmen have pursued since the first quarter of this century. It was in the year 1820 that the merchants of London formulated a noteworthy petition praying that every restrictive regulation of trade—not imposed on account of the revenue,—together with all duties of a protective character, might be at once repealed. The leading merchants of Edinburgh sent up a similar petition, and a com-

[1] If we exclude the Irish population (nearly 7,000,000), whose condition was very different from that of Great Britain, this would give a higher rate.

mittee was appointed in Parliament to investigate the wishes of the petitioners of the Northern and Southern capitals; which committee finally brought in a report thoroughly in harmony with the free trade principles of the merchants. In the following year William Huskisson, who was President of the Board of Trade, proposed the first measures of commercial reform, and since then one by one the restrictions upon our trade have been removed. Indeed, it may be said that with Huskisson a marked alteration came over our commercial policy, and protection gave way to free trade. It is true that he was not able to do much at first, for when he offered to abolish the import duty on raw cotton if manufacturers would consent to give up the export duty, the manufacturers declined. When again he attempted to free the silk manufacture in Spitalfields from various restrictions, including the settlement of wages by magistrates, no less than 11,000 journeymen petitioned against the proposal, and it was dropped. But he was successful in one of the most important measures he proposed, namely, the gradual alteration of the old Navigation Acts, though these were not finally repealed until 1849.[1] In 1824 he reduced the duty on raw and spun silk and lowered the import duty on wool, removing also the prohibition on its export; he also in 1823 passed the Reciprocity of Duties Bill, by which English and foreign ships had equal advantages in England whenever foreign nations allowed the same to English vessels in their ports. He also threw open the commerce of our colonies to other nations, though under certain restrictions. Hence it will be seen that he made considerable progress in forwarding the new policy,[2] and his accidental death in 1830,

[1] They were not repealed for the *coasting* trade till 1854.
[2] Most of his reforms were embodied in the budgets of 1823-25, when Robinson was Chancellor of the Exchequer.

at the opening of the Liverpool and Manchester railway, was a great loss to his country.

§ 75. **Cobden and the Corn Laws.**—Whilst these reforms were going on, there was begun that memorable free trade agitation which ended in the repeal of the Corn Laws, and in bringing to the front the name of Richard Cobden. A series of bad harvests, resulting in the usual riots and agitation that always accompanied them in those days, made people think that something should be done in relaxing the import duties[1] upon grain; and in 1828 the "sliding scale" of duties on corn was introduced, by which, as the price of corn rose, the duty fell, and as the price fell, the duty rose. The full repeal of the Corn Laws, however, did not take place until quite twenty years afterwards, nor was the Anti-Corn Law League formed till 1838; but at last, owing to the efforts of Richard Cobden, John Bright, and other economists and politicians of note, Sir Robert Peel[2] brought in a bill in 1846 by which the duties on corn were reduced every year, until at last, in 1849, they ceased to exist. As the Navigation Acts also were finally repealed in the same year, and the Customs Bill further reduced or abolished duties[3] on imports, especially of food and raw material, the year 1849 may be taken as marking the final decision of England to adopt the policy of free trade.

[1] By the Act 55 Geo. III., c. 26, in 1815 foreign corn was not admitted into England till wheat was at 80s. a qr. It was hoped that this device would raise prices, but agricultural distress still prevailed. By the 3 Geo. IV., c. 60, 70s. was substituted for 80s. per qr.

[2] The failure of the potato crop in Ireland in 1845, and the consequent famine, finally convinced Peel of the necessity of abolishing these laws.

[3] In 1842 Peel had reduced or abolished duties on 750 out of 1200 of our imports.

§ 76. **The Revolution in Transit.**—Meanwhile another change, almost as important as the Industrial Revolution, was approaching—the Revolution in the means of transit. Of course, it is impossible here to go into details about those great inventions by which the power of steam, which had been employed for many years in working machinery in mills and factories, was now applied as a motive force for locomotion. We can only say that the first railway—that between Stockton and Darlington—was opened in 1825, and a much more important one between Manchester and Liverpool in 1830. After the railways came the steamers, and in 1838 the first ocean passages made by steamships were accomplished by the *Great Western* from Liverpool, and the *Sirius* from Cork.[1] Next came the great discovery of the electric telegraph, the patent for the needle telegraph having been taken out in 1837, though the Electric Telegraph Company, whose object it was to bring the new inventions into general use, was not founded till 1846. The reform of the Post Office, by the introduction of the penny post in 1840, was another step towards freedom of communication and intercourse. When, therefore, we look at the remarkable changes brought about by these discoveries and inventions, and when we consider the enormous facilities which they have given to the development of modern commerce, and to rapid communication both between individuals and nations, we may well regard the few years in which they were introduced as marking a period which deserves to be called the Commercial

---

[1] A steamer, *The Comet*, made by Henry Bell was plying on the River Clyde as early as 1812 ; and Fulton, in America, had made one in 1811.

THE ERA OF FREE TRADE. 107

Revolution of the Nineteenth Century. One more great fact remains to be mentioned which is of more than even national importance—the opening of the Suez Canal in 1869, which has brought the East and West into closer and closer communication, and has been the means of opening up new markets that were previously only with difficulty accessible.

§ 77. **Commercial Crises.**—It must not, however, be supposed that the progress of industry and commerce has gone on since 1815 without any checks. There have been serious hindrances in many respects, and commercial crises have not been infrequent. Indeed, very soon after the conclusion of the Continental War, a severe commercial crisis passed over this country. It happened partly because during the war our manufacturers had accumulated vast stocks of manufactured products, and could not get rid of them as quickly as they expected, owing to the financial exhaustion of those countries whom they expected to be their customers, and partly also because foreign countries sought to protect their own almost ruined industries by imposing almost prohibitive duties upon English manufactures. The harvests of 1816 and 1817 were also very bad in England, and these, added to the causes just mentioned, produced a very severe crisis, which reached its worst point in 1819. Once again, in 1825 a second crisis followed, caused by the too rapid importation of raw products that had been bought at a very high price, and by financial follies in speculation in the trade with the Spanish American colonies,[1] that seemed to recall the days of the South Sea Bubble. In fact, this panic is often called the Second South

[1] These colonies required capital to work their silver mines, and this led to heavy speculation by English capitalists.

Sea Bubble.[1] Ten years afterwards, in 1836 to 1839, another crisis occurred, owing chiefly to the formation of numerous joint-stock banks and other companies, together with extravagant speculation in corn and tea. During the forties, however, our commercial condition continued to improve, and capital was rapidly accumulated till the bad harvest of 1846, combined with speculations in grain, and the high price of cotton, caused another period of disaster, in which the cotton industry in particular was severely damaged. The speculations in railways were also remarkable at this time, no less than £700,000,000 being raised in railway capital in 1847. The country, however, recovered once more, and with the discoveries of gold in California and Australia in 1851, a renewed activity was seen in all branches of trade. As the supplies of gold increased, English exports increased also, since they were eagerly taken, especially by Australia, in return for the precious metals. Nevertheless, before very long another crisis broke upon the commercial community (1857), having its origin in North America, but which extended over the whole commercial world and proved very prejudicial to English interests on account of the close connection between our country and the United States. This time our iron and textile industries were specially affected; factories were closed, and blast furnaces extinguished, and the greatest distress prevailed amongst the working-classes. But once more the nation recovered as usual; and for another few years continued to prosper, till

[1] Much of the harm done was caused by the unchecked issue of £1 and £2 notes by the smaller banks, who had thus established an extensive paper currency, which they could not redeem when a run came. An Act was therefore passed to prevent the issue of these notes, though it was not applied to Scotland or Ireland, owing to the opposition aroused in these countries.

the cotton industry was for a second time almost ruined by the effects of the Slavery War between the Northern and Southern States of America. A "cotton famine" occurred in Lancashire, when 800,000 wage-earners were deprived of their livelihood. This caused an increase of cotton-growing in India, which has continued since that time.

§ 78. **Other Commercial Crises.** — But once again this industry recovered from what seemed to be a very, severe blow, and the close of the American War in 1865 even gave a further impetus to new business, while at the same time considerable developments took place in our trade with China, India, and Australia. But the very next year the sudden and unexpected failure of the great bill-broking firm of Overend, Gurney & Co. caused much panic, not only in financial but in industrial circles, though the ordinary symptoms of crisis were fortunately not apparent in the trade returns, and for some years our prosperity continued to increase till a crisis of truly international magnitude occurred in 1873. It was felt from New York to Moscow, and affected the trade, industry, and agriculture of all intervening countries. It was due to some extent to the great financial inflation which took place within the German Empire after the payment of £200,000,000 indemnity by the French to their conquerors, while a similar inflation prevailed in the United States, owing to the rapid growth of business and the extension of railways after the Civil War. England escaped much of the severity of this international crisis (1873),[1] but soon afterwards suffered from agricultural depression, and has continued to do so since, owing to the ever increasing development of American agriculture. Dur-

[1] Though two great failures—that of Collie & Co. in 1875, and the Glasgow Bank in 1878—showed that there was some uneasiness.

ing the last twenty years the two most severe periods of crisis have taken place in 1882 and 1890, the former connected with the failure of the Union Générale of France[1] combined with the low prices and general stagnation of trade in Great Britain, which lasted till 1888 ; and the latter due to the extravagant speculation, especially in South American securities, which terminated in the difficulties experienced by the well-known firm of Baring Brothers and the panic which followed the discovery of their unsafe situation. More recently still the increasingly protective McKinley Tariff adopted by the United States has had a depressing effect upon many British industries.

The fact that so many crises have taken place with such almost unfailing regularity during the whole of this century, shows that the modern system of home and foreign commerce does not rest upon an entirely secure basis ; but how they are to be remedied it does not come within the scope of this book to state. It is sufficient to point out that they have occurred in the past, and that, under the present industrial and commercial system, they will probably continue to occur in the future.

§ 79. **The Bank of England.**—But throughout all these periods of crisis the Bank of England has stood firm ever since the time when it resumed payment of its notes in cash (1821). It was somewhat in danger during the crisis of 1825, and received Government help at that time, and since then two Acts have been passed in reference to its charter, which deserve our attention at this point. The first was the Bank Charter Act of 1833, which attempted to

---

[1] The Union Générale was a scheme for establishing a great banking society supported by Roman Catholics only. It lasted from 1878 to 1882, and then collapsed.

stop runs upon the bank, by enacting that its notes should be made legal tender, so that the country banks might be able to meet a panic with notes instead of gold. A deduction of £120,000 a year was to be made from the sum allowed to the bank for its management of the National Debt, but in return for this a quarter of the sum due (£14,686,800) was paid back. About this time[1] also the directors began to act upon the great principle that the amount of paper issued and of specie kept in stock should have a certain proportion to one another, the ratio being 3 to 1, and the bank published a general statement of its condition every quarter. In spite of this measure, the bank was occasionally in difficulty, and nearly stopped payment in 1839, so that Sir Robert Peel in 1844 proposed the second Bank Charter Act, the object of which was to regulate the issue of notes. It enacted that the bank should not issue more than £14,000,000 in notes unless a corresponding amount of specie was kept in stock; and furthermore, that no new banks that should be established after the measure became law were to issue their own notes, nor were the old banks to increase their issue. Since then no further legislation has been necessary, and large numbers of joint-stock banks have been formed, some of which hold a position which almost rivals that of the Bank of England.[2] Nevertheless

[1] McCulloch, *Comm. Dict.*

[2] We may here mention that the Bank of Scotland that was established by an Act of the Scottish Parliament in 1695 was allowed to issue £1 notes in 1704, and still continues to do so. After the union of England and Scotland it undertook the re-coinage with great success, and established an office in London in 1857. The Bank of Ireland was established in 1783 by a charter in consequence of a request from the Irish Parliament, with the same constitutional privileges as the Bank of England. But Bank of Ireland notes are not legal tender.

the second Bank Charter Act has had to be suspended three times since its enactment; namely, in the crises of 1844, 1857, and 1866. But an eminent authority assures us that "there has really been no *panic* in England since 1866."[1]

[1] W. Fowler in his most valuable and practical article on "Crises" in the *Dict. of Pol. Econ.* His views should be compared with those of H. M. Hyndman, *Commercial Crises of the 19th Century.*

CHAPTER XVI.

CHANGES IN THE NATURE OF OUR TRADE IN THE PRESENT CENTURY—EASTERN AFFAIRS.

§ 80. **Direction and Extent of our Trade.**—Having thus traced the progress of English trade for nearly three centuries, from the days of the Elizabethan sailors to the great financiers and foreign merchants of the present time, we may now glance briefly at some of the changes which have taken place in its direction and extent. In the earliest periods of our trade, wool and tin were our chief exports, and then manufactured woollen cloths came into prominence. Similarly in more modern times, owing to the Industrial Revolution and the introduction of machinery and steam power, our greatest exports have been in textile goods and in manufactures of metals. In textile goods woollen cloths formed at the end of the 18th century by far the larger portion of our exports, cotton goods being only a little over half their value; but in 1802 the value of cotton goods surpassed that of woollens, and at the present time is considerably more important. At the beginning of this century, iron, steel, and copper were only just beginning to be of much importance, but since then they have come to form one of the largest items of our foreign trade.

In the imports we see corresponding developments. In 1701 Liverpool imported only 68,400 bales of raw cotton;

in 1810 the number rose to 182,000; and at the present time the value of raw cotton imported is over £36,000,000 annually. We might notice in passing that a change has taken place in the source from which our cotton supply is derived. In 1791 the largest portion came from Brazil, the next largest from the West Indies, while only the insignificant number of 91 bales came from the United States. But in twenty years the cotton crops of the States had become so important that they far surpassed both the West Indies and Brazil in the amount grown, and still do so; though now the East Indies and Egypt supply a fair quantity.

After the cotton import, that of raw wool stands highest, being about £21,000,000 in value annually, a large proportion of which comes from our own colonies. Our imports from the East have also attained far more importance in the last hundred years, the imports of raw silk, indigo, tea, coffee, and spices forming a large proportion of the trade which we have, as it were, taken out of the hands of the French and Dutch. Then again, in the last few years of the 18th century and the first few years of the 19th, our trade with the West Indies and South America held a higher position in regard to the general volume than it does at present. Jamaica, Demerara, and other British possessions in the West Indies supplied at that time almost half the sugar consumed on the Continent of Europe, while between 1788 and 1805 their production of sugar was almost doubled. In the first ten years of the 19th century the value of the total imports from the West Indian colonies was about £8,000,000, of which £7,000,000 represented sugar.

§ 81. **Recent Changes in our Trade.** — But in the next two decades another change took place in the cotton industry. England, which had formerly had almost the monopoly of manufacture and sale on the Continent and in America, has begun to feel rather severely the competition of continental and American rivals, while the cotton factories of Bombay are at the same time causing much anxious thought to Lancashire manufacturers. On the other hand, the woollen industries have been increasing, partly owing to the rapid increase of the production of raw wool in the British colonies. Meanwhile the manufactures of iron, steel, and hardware generally have continued to increase, and the export of raw iron and other metals has also progressed, while the export of coal has increased most of all. A considerable increase also has been shown in the export of jute[1] and refined sugar.[2]

Among the imports, cotton, as we said above, still holds the first place among raw materials, and is followed by wool and metals. But all these are far surpassed by the immense quantity of grain and flour which are now imported to the value of £55,000,000 annually, and if we include animals, butter, tea, fruits, and other food materials, the total import under this head comes to £135,000,000.

But perhaps the most noticeable changes in the direction of our trade have been seen in regard to our colonial possessions. About the end of the last century Europe received from England about as much as England exported to all other parts of the world; about 1860 only one-third of the total exports of England were sent to the Continent, while the other two-thirds went to our colonial possessions and to other distant foreign countries, but at the present time our colonial possessions receive about one-third of our exports. In the fifty years 1840-89, the total value

[1] Farrer, *Free Trade* v. *Fair Trade*, p. 335. [2] *Ib.* p. 259.

of our export trade has increased quite sixfold, and that, too, although many goods (*e.g.*, cottons and woollens) are now produced more cheaply than before, and therefore the same value in figures represents a larger volume of goods exported. Our colonies alone now take in British exports nearly twice the value of our total export trade as it existed fifty years ago.[1]

§ 82. **Eastern Trade : China.**[2]—Our trade with the East has also largely increased during the last half century, but in its interests we waged two wars with China, which some people have thought to be unjust. The first Chinese War occurred in 1840, because the Chinese Government forbade the use of opium, which British traders insisted on introducing. The war was a short one, and resulted in the acquisition of Hong Kong for England, the opening of five new treaty ports to our ships, and the payment of nearly four and a half millions sterling to England, and one and a quarter million to British merchants. The second war arose in 1856, and was caused by the Chinese seizing a smuggling ship that carried the British flag. Lord Palmerston went into the struggle with the motto, "Our country, right or wrong;" but his Government was in consequence violently attacked by Peelites, Whigs, Conservatives, and the Manchester Peace Party, led by Bright and Cobden. The Chinese, however, were beaten, and five more ports were thrown open to commerce, while special privileges were granted to British subjects and Christianity was tolerated. Since then, except a slight misunderstanding caused in 1859 by the stoppage of British and French ambassadors on their way to Pekin, China has given no more trouble.

§ 83. **Eastern Trade : Egypt.**—We have had, how-

[1] Cf. my *Commerce in Europe*, p. 223-5.
[2] The quite modern growth of the trade and manufactures of Japan should also be included.

ever, to intervene for commercial and political purposes in Egypt in late years. Since the Suez Canal runs through that country and forms part of our ocean highway to India, it is absolutely necessary that it should be kept open for traffic both of a commercial and military character. England had not the good sense to acquire a large proprietary interest in the canal when it was first cut, but the sagacity of the late Earl of Beaconsfield [1] remedied this fault in 1875, when the Government bought from the Khedive his 400,000 shares in the canal for £4,000,000, and thus made England the largest shareholder. Then in 1879, Egypt, having become practically bankrupt, was handed over to the dual control of England and France, the Khedive being only a nominal ruler, and thus our interest in the country was still more firmly established. Since then this land has fallen still more under English influence, owing to the events of 1882. An Egyptian officer, named Arabi Pasha, headed a national rising against the foreign influence of European powers, but was defeated by our troops and exiled to Ceylon. France had refused to help England in this conflict and in another which followed when the Arabs of the Soudan revolted in 1883 under the Mahdi, and thus she practically withdrew from her share of the dual control, though she still lays claim to it. Hence, during the last ten years England has been really the ruling power in Egypt, and as long as she wishes to retain her Indian Empire she will have to continue to exercise an influence in Egyptian affairs. Her position there is entirely due to her commercial and colonial developments in the East.

[1] This great statesman, who clearly perceived that England was a great Eastern as well as a great European power, also procured Cyprus for us from Turkey in 1878, thus giving us a further stronghold on the way to India.

CHAPTER XVII.

MODERN COLONIAL DEVELOPMENT—WITH AN APPENDIX OF
THE POSSESSIONS OF THE BRITISH EMPIRE.

§ 84. **Our Second Colonial Empire.**—It is often forgotten how comparatively recent is the acquisition of our present colonial possessions. Few people realise that, with the exception of one or two provinces of India and Canada, and a very few of the West Indian islands, all of them have been acquired within the last hundred years. The fact is that the breaking off of the American colonies in 1783 marks the dividing line between our first colonial empire and our second. At that time our empire suffered a loss which seemed as if it would be almost fatal, but as a matter of fact it has presented hardly any hindrance to our colonial progress. As has been pointed out by various writers, England found compensation elsewhere, while at the same time our purely commercial connections with the United States were not very seriously injured, as they continued to deal with us very much as before, owing to the fact that England was the only country which could supply the manufactures they needed, and has ever since remained the best market for their agricultural products. The trade between England and North America was, and has been, essentially a natural and not an artificial trade; and being natural, it has suffered very little from political disturbances.

MODERN COLONIAL DEVELOPMENT. 119

Meanwhile, soon after the loss of her American colonies, England began to compensate herself by obtaining others in various other portions of the globe, taking them for nearly a quarter of a century almost entirely by conquest. Thus we obtained Ceylon (1796); Guiana (1803); the Cape of Good Hope (1806), all of which originally belonged to the Dutch; Trinidad (1797) was taken from Spain; Mauritius (1810) and many of the West Indian islands from France; while at the same time we were increasing our hold upon West Africa, and rapidly extending our dominion in India. Moreover, colonisation of quite a different type was being carried on in Australia and in Canada. There are, in fact, four chief lines of reconstruction and fresh development to be noticed in the history of our recent acquisitions. These lines of development are to be found: (1) in the West Indies; (2) in Australia; (3) in Canada; (4) in Africa.[1]

§ 85. **The West Indies.**—These were for some time the centre of our colonial interest, especially after they had been secured to us by Rodney's great naval victory [2] over the French in the West Indies in 1782, and they rapidly became a source of increasing wealth till, at the close of the last century, the West Indian influence in the city of London and in Bristol became a factor of considerable commercial importance. The chief islands of the various groups which form the West Indies are, commercially speaking, Jamaica, Trinidad, and Barbadoes, to which we may add the continental settlement of British Guiana. Their development continued for many years to be closely identified with the sugar industry, but a severe blow was dealt to their prosperity by the invention of beet sugar and the abolition of slavery. The use of beet sugar in Europe, encouraged

[1] Compare chap. vi. of Caldecott's *English Colonisation*.
[2] When he defeated the French Admiral De Grasse, in a fight between Dominica and Guadeloupe, April 5th-10th, 1782.

as it has been by bounties given by European Governments to the manufacturers and growers of beetroot, has extended enormously within the last fifty years. Only 95,000 tons of beet sugar were produced in 1849 as compared with 3,630,000 tons in 1890, in which last year it considerably exceeded the amount of cane sugar manufactured. Thus the West Indies, which had practically a monopoly of the sugar supply of Europe, now found this monopoly entirely ruined,[1] while the change in its labour system has been—to put it mildly—by no means so beneficial as the promoters of the anti-slavery agitation fondly hoped.[2] Hence our West Indian colonies are now in a somewhat critical position.

§ 86. **The Australian Colonies.**—The next group of colonies that demands our attention is that of Australia and New Zealand. These are colonies in a totally different sense from the West Indies, because they are the homes of thousands of English settlers who have gone out there to found a new state beyond the seas (cf. page 25). They and Canada form, in fact, a Greater Britain in a far truer sense than any other colony can be said to do so. It was, of course, the adventurous voyages of Captain Cook that first attracted attention towards these new fields of colonisation, and in 1788 our first settlement was made on the shores of Australia, in Port Jackson, but our first settlers were only convicts, and for a long time the system was in operation of sending to Australia men and women who had proved themselves too criminal to be tolerated at home.[3] But

[1] Cf. Caldecott, *English Colonisation*, pp. 93-95, for a summary of causes of the decline of the West Indies; and Farrer, *Free Trade* v. *Fair Trade*, ch. 48, for the sugar trade.

[2] Slavery was abolished in the British domains in 1833, when £20,000,000 was given to the planters as compensation.

[3] In 1821 New South Wales had a population of 30,000, of whom three-fourths were convicts.

these somewhat undesirable settlers were followed gradually by streams of free men, and the new colonies—largely owing to the suggestions of Edward Wakefield[1]—continued to attract other emigrants by offering them facilities for passage and for acquiring land upon their arrival. So the stream of colonisation went on for some time, though the number of colonists was never very large, till in 1851 a new and unrivalled attraction was found in the discovery of the Ballarat goldfields. The discovery of gold attracted vast numbers of emigrants, many being of an adventurous and energetic character, and although most of them did not succeed in making their fortunes in gold-mining, they settled down to other industries, and began to develop the various resources of the country.[2] The most notable of these has been sheep-farming, for the country was found to be particularly suitable for the production of wool. The number of sheep rose from only 25,000 in 1810 to 290,000 in 1821, and they are now counted in millions. The first of our colonies was New South Wales—from which Victoria (1851) and Queensland (1859) were cut out. South Australia was a separate colony from its beginning (1836), and so was Western Australia. New Zealand was occupied by us in 1840, and a New Zealand Company was formed, while a Government connection was made with it by the appointment of a governor in the same year. "Of all our colonies, New Zealand may be said to be almost the only case of a purely industrial emigration colony of British people. It was neither sought as a refuge from religious or political oppression like New England, nor founded as a

[1] Caldecott, p. 98.
[2] There has been a similar rush to the goldfields of Western Australia in the last two years (1894-1896).

convict settlement like New South Wales, nor stimulated into sudden prosperity by a rush for gold like Victoria. It never knew any slavery or coolie system like the West Indies, nor does it contain an important foreign element like the Cape Colony and Canada." [1] At the same time it may be said that the history of all our Australian colonies is of an industrial character, as they have been developed entirely by emigrants of British origin, working upon well known industrial lines.

§ 87. **The Canadian Dominion.**—Fortunately the loss of our thirteen American colonies did not involve the loss of the dominions which we had recently taken from the French (see p. 85). Newfoundland, Nova Scotia, and New Brunswick remained unaffected, and so also did the province of Quebec, though the Quebec Act [2] of 1774 very nearly caused a rupture with that particular province. The French population was only about 65,000 when we took over these territories, though it has since increased very largely, so much so that this has been called the most successful colony that ever issued from the French nation, although it has been developed under British influences and amid British surroundings. The original province was divided into Upper and Lower Canada in 1791, the former being chiefly British and the latter containing the largest proportion of French settlers, and in spite of the attempts of the United States to make them unite with the "stars and stripes" in 1812, they remained loyal to England. Upper and Lower Canada were reunited in 1841, and a "responsible" govern-

[1] Caldecott, *English Colonisation*, p. 99.
[2] It was passed in order to conciliate the French settlers. It established the Roman Catholic Church and restored the old French system generally, being very favourable to French Canadians.

MODERN COLONIAL DEVELOPMENT. 123

ment was granted to the colony. This may be taken as the inauguration of the present system of self-government for our larger colonies, and marks a step of great historical importance. In 1867 the whole group, including Nova Scotia and New Brunswick, was united into the Dominion of Canada, and since then divisions of the lands lying to the west of the older settlements have gradually been made, until now we have the separate provinces of Manitoba, British Columbia, the North-West territories and Prince Edward Island. In these colonies again, we find, as in Australia, a steady stream of genuine British settlers, who have proceeded upon industrial lines and are forming a most important industrial community.

§ 88. **Our African Possessions.**—The history of our colonies in Africa is largely one of conquest. The English took possession of the Cape by force in 1795, restored it to the Dutch in 1803, captured it again in 1806, and had it finally ceded to them by the Great Peace of 1815. When it came into our hands, we found that there were not more than 10,000 Dutch settled there, and that trade was totally unorganised, so much so that wool brought down from the farmers of the interior to the beach sometimes lay there unsold until the wind scattered it. In striking contrast to this, we may notice that the value of wool now exported from the Cape is worth nearly £2,000,000 annually. It is impossible here to go into the history of our relations with the Dutch; it must be sufficient to remark that there still seems to be an unfortunate difficulty in working in harmony with them as our fellow-colonists, and that a still greater difficulty presents itself in regard to the native races, who, so far from decreasing in numbers, and declining in power before the advance of the whites (as the Maoris in New

Zealand or the Indians in America), have continued to increase and prosper to an almost embarrassing extent. Only one person out of six in the African colonies is a white. Numerous and costly wars have been waged with the native tribes of South Africa, of which the latest and most important was the Zulu War of 1879 and 1880. Disturbances have also occurred with the Dutch, which have resulted in the formation of two practically independent states, the Orange Free State and the South African Republic (or Transvaal), though it may be hoped that the possible incorporation of these two last states into one great South African dominion is only a question of time. This will need, however, considerably more tact and intelligence than has hitherto been shown by British and African statesmen in dealing with South African affairs.[1] Besides these states and the provinces of Cape Colony, Natal, and Bechuanaland, and the other territories which go to make up our South African colonies, a great extension of British influence is being made at the present time by the old method of chartered companies, who are proceeding in many respects upon much the same lines as the old East India Company did in its earliest days. Such are the British South African Company, now developing Matabeleland and Mashonaland, the East African Company, with its chief port at Mombasa, and the Royal Niger Company, which carries on trade in the basin of the Niger. It is extremely interesting to notice how this old method of a chartered company is still being used to extend British trade and influence.

As regards the development of African trade, it should be noticed that it has received a great impetus from the discovery of diamonds in large quantities, and more recently

[1] This remark was written early in 1893, but there is no reason to alter it in 1896.

still of gold; so that emgirants are being attracted thither in the same manner, though not quite to the same extent as they were formerly attracted to the Australian gold fields.

§ 89. **Various Colonies : Colonial Tariffs.**—These, then, are the four directions in which our colonial empire has mainly extended since the great War of American Independence. Besides the colonies here mentioned we have since then obtained various other small and scattered possessions in different parts of the world, a list of which will be found in the appendix to this chapter. The most important of them commercially have been the Straits Settlements, including Singapore (purchased in 1819), which is now a great emporium for tropical produce on the one hand, and for British and native manufactures on the other; and Hong Kong, which we gained after the first Chinese War, and which is the main centre for our commerce with China, having a total trade of £20,000,000 sterling per annum, though this is only half that of Singapore. An enumeration of our other possessions will be found in the appendix here given, which includes the whole of our colonial empire, and forms a fitting conclusion to the story of our commercial development.

Some mention, however, must be made of the commercial policy of the colonies towards their mother country.[1] It is characterised by an unfortunate spirit of protectionism. When the right of self-government was conceded to our possessions, it carried with it the right of raising revenue in any manner that might seem best to colonial administrators, even if this involved duties on British products. Now, Canada received the right of self-government in 1840, the Australian colonies between 1850 and '60, and the

[1] Cf. Prof. Bastable's chapter (10) on "Colonial and other Tariffs" in his *Commerce of Nations*, p. 106.

Cape in 1872; and with it they received also full power over their own commercial policy. At first, they adopted the system of low import duties, merely for revenue purposes; but gradually protectionist measures gained ground, till these low revenue tariffs have develeped into complicated customs systems with duties upon most kinds of manufactured goods. The colonies of Australasia, with the exception of New South Wales, have all adopted a rigorous protective system. So has Canada. The Cape has also raised its duties since 1872. India almost alone, the greatest dependency of all, follows the commercial policy of Great Britain; and, in consequence, meets with her reward in the growth of Indian trade. Some colonies even employ export duties, which are regarded as really a charge on the land which produces the taxed articles. On the whole, the reactionary policy of our colonies has not done so much harm as might be expected, since they cannot affect the nature of their trade, which must consist in the export of raw materials and food products in exchange for manufactures—at any rate for some time to come. But such a policy does no good and merely hampers an otherwise flourishing trade; and it is not unreasonable that Great Britain should be disappointed that her colonies do not follow her own more liberal and rational system.

THE BRITISH EMPIRE.

A LIST OF OUR POSSESSIONS AND COLONIES, WITH DATE AND MANNER OF ACQUISITION, AND THEIR COMMERCIAL PRODUCTS.

§ 90. **Europe.**—Our possessions here are small in number and extent, but strong in position, and are important as maintaining the route to India and the supremacy of the ocean. They are (1) **Gibraltar**, captured by Sir G. Rooke in 1704, and assigned to England by the Treaty of Utrecht in 1713. (2) **Malta** and the Maltese Islands, captured in the French War in 1800. Naval station, strongly fortified. *Exports* cotton, grain, potatoes, and fruit. (3) **Cyprus**, granted by Turkey in 1878; *produces* cotton, wine, wool, silk, grain, sponges, raisins, lead, and building stones; *population*, 186,000.

§ 91. **Asia.**—Here our possessions are both extensive and valuable, consisting of the Indian Empire, Ceylon, and several smaller settlements and stations. **Aden**, a rocky peninsula in South Arabia, captured in 1839; fortress and coaling station on steamer line from Suez to Bombay. **Perim**, acquired 1855; small island, 4 miles long at entrance of Red Sea; harbour and lighthouse; fortified. **Kuria-Muria Islands**, off the coast of Oman, Arabia; acquired in 1854 by the Bombay Government as a telegraph station. **Socotra Island**, a large island at entrance of Gulf of Aden; annexed in 1886; *products*, aloes, dates, figs, dyes, etc. **Mauritius**, island in Indian Ocean, Crown colony, captured from French 1810; fertile; *chief industry*, sugar-cane growing; also *exports* cotton, coffee, indigo, tortoiseshell, ebony, vanilla. Dependent on the Government of Mauritius are the **Seychelles, Rodriguez, Amirante, Diego Garcia**, and **Chagos Islands**. The Seychelles *export* cocoa-nuts and cocoa-nut oil, sperm, vanilla, coffee, and cloves. The others chiefly abound with turtles, but the Chagos Islands and Diego Garcia *export* also cocoa-nut oil, fruit, poultry, and vegetables. **Ceylon**, captured from Dutch 1796; a large island, only one-fourth less than Ireland; Crown colony; *exports* coffee chiefly, but also tea, cinchona, cocoa-nut and other palms; grain, rice, and cinnamon also cultivated; precious stones, iron, plumbago, nitre, and salt found, and pearl fishery carried on. The **Maldive Islands**, a group 500 miles west of Ceylon, are tributary to Government of Ceylon, and *export* cocoa-nuts, etc. Of the **Andaman** and **Nicobar** islands the former are used as a native convict settlement (Port Blair); they are densely wooded.

§ 92. The **Indian Empire** consists of the following Provinces of British India—*viz.*, Bengal, N.W. Provinces and Oude, Punjab, Central Provinces, Lower Burmah (acquired 1826 and 1852), Upper Burmah (1886), Assam, Madras, Bombay, and Berar; also, 800 native states, large and small, subject to the Government. The chief *products* of India are wheat, cotton, indigo, opium, tea, tobacco, sugar, rice, and tropical fruits; timber, especially teak; silk, wool, ivory, iron, coal, salt, lead, and, in Burmah, precious stones, rice, and timber. The population is about eight times that of Great Britain, and the area of the British Provinces alone is more than ten times that of Great Britain.

§ 93. The **Straits Settlements** include :—The island of Singapore, acquired 1819, which, besides being a commercial emporium for the far East, *exports* guttapercha, caoutchouc, sago, spices, tin, canes, etc., from the surrounding districts; **Penang**, bought in 1785, *exports* spices; **Province Wellesley**, acquired in 1800 in order to stop piracy, *exports* poultry, cattle, and colonial produce; **Malacca**, captured from the Dutch in 1795, *exports* gold-dust, tin, ivory, tapioca, and canes; **Perak, Selangor**, and **Sungei Ujong** are native states, " protected " since about 1876; and Jeleba (1885), Negri Sembilan (1886), and Pahang (1888) are also subject to the Government of the Straits Settlements. The **Cocos** or **Keeling Islands** *export* cocoa-nuts. All the above are included in the Government of the Straits Settlements, which was formed into one Government in 1867.

Labuan Island, purchased and occupied in 1848, *exports* sago, beeswax, camphor, hides, rattans, tortoiseshell, and trepang, and has a valuable coal mine.

British North Borneo is the property of an English chartered company (1877), and a protectorate was proclaimed over it in 1888,

THE BRITISH EMPIRE. 129

as well as over **Brunei** and **Sarawak**; it has immense mineral resources—coal, iron, gold, diamonds, antimony, quicksilver, and *exports* these, together with sago, pepper, indigo, arrowroot, spices, drugs, dyes, caoutchouc, and guttapercha.

Hong Kong Island, with Kowloon (1860) and the Lema Islands, was ceded by China in 1842, is a Crown colony, and *exports* tea, silk, and Chinese produce generally, and is a great commercial emporium for British trade with the East. Military and Naval Station, our "Eastern Gibraltar."

§ 94. AUSTRALASIA.—Our possessions here include the island continent of Australia, with the large islands of New Zealand and Tasmania, and many smaller islands.

AUSTRALIA is divided into the following colonies, which are colonies of emigration, not of conquest (p. 24):—**New South Wales,** settled 1788; **Victoria,** a separate colony since 1851; **South Australia** formed in 1836; **Queensland,** in 1859; **Western Australia,** 1829. These colonies have each a responsible government, but the **Northern Territory** is under a president, subject to South Australia. The chief *products* of all the colonies are gold and wool; also wheat, wine, fruit, copper, coal, iron; and in Queensland, much of which is semi-tropical, sugar and cotton. Good pasture for sheep in most parts. Most gold is found in Victoria.

Tasmania, an island only a quarter less than Ireland, discovered by Tasman, a Dutchman, in 1642; settled as a penal colony from England, 1803; separated from Government of New South Wales, 1825; representative government established, 1853; responsible government, 1871; fertile and well wooded; *exports* wool, tin, gold, fruit, timber.

New Zealand is a group of three islands; total area rather larger than Great Britain; discovered by Tasman, in 1642; rediscovered by Captain Cook, 1770; colony, 1840; independent, 1842; *products*, gold, coal, iron, timber, kauri gum, wool, hides, wheat, meat, flax.

In **New Guinea** Britain has taken possession since 1885 of an area of some 86,000 square miles, chiefly in the south; it is under a governor since 1888 as a Crown colony; rich in tropical products; and gold is also found. Adjacent islands S. of 8° S. lat. are English. **Norfolk Island,** visited by Cook, 1774, was made a penal settlement, 1787 to 1856; now under protection of Governor of New South Wales, and settled by descendants of mutineers of the *Bounty*. **Lord Howe Island**, taken 1856, is under no authority. The **Chatham Islands** (1840) and **Kermadec Islands** are under Government of New Zealand, and like the **Auckland Islands, Campbell Islands**, and **Macquarie Islands**, are visited by whalers for seals and provisions. **Pitcairn Island**, settled in 1790 by mutineers of *Bounty*, is rarely visited, nor is **Antipodes Island**. England exercises since 1889 a protectorate over the **Union** and **Phœnix** groups, north of Fiji, some of which grow cocoa-nuts and others contain guano. The **Fiji Islands** were ceded to England by the King, in 1874; population, 120,000; well wooded; luxuriant vegetation; *produce* sugar, copra, fruits, maize, cotton, coffee. The **Rotumah Islands**, annexed 1881, are subject to Governor of Fiji, and the **Tonga Islands**, annexed in 1881, have a British resident, but a native monarchy.

§ 95. AMERICA.—Here our possessions are very numerous, both on the Continent and the adjacent islands. They include the **Dominion of Canada**, taken mostly in 1763 from French, which contains the following provinces:—Ontario (1763), Quebec (1763), Nova Scotia and Cape Breton Island (1713), New Brunswick (1761), Prince Edward Island (1763), and entered the Dominion 1870. Manitoba belonged originally to the Hudson Bay Company, and so did British Columbia and the North-West Territories. British Columbia was made a separate colony with Vancouver Island in 1858, but entered the Dominion in 1870, as did Manitoba and the Territories. The Hudson Bay Company (founded 1670, for trading purposes) ceded the North-West Territories for one and a half million dollars. The Dominion *exports* timber, petroleum, copper, fish, furs, skins, agricultural and dairy produce, cattle, and grain.

Newfoundland is not in the Dominion; ceded by France 1713; *chief industry* is fishing, but copper and coal exist. **Labrador** is subject to Government of Newfoundland. All the Canadian colonies have responsible governments of their own.

In Central America we possess **British Honduras**, ceded by Spain in 1783; Crown colony; *exports* chiefly logwood and mahogany; also coffee and sugar and dyes. In South America we have **British Guiana**, taken in 1803; *exports* sugar, rum, timber, drugs, gums, and cochineal; has governor and representative government.

§ 96. Our possessions in the WEST INDIES are numerous, and include :—The **Bermuda Islands**; Colonised 1611, after Somers had been wrecked there in 1609; representative government, naval station; *products* are fruit, potatoes, timber (cedar), and arrowroot. The **Bahamas**; colonised twice by settlers, 1629 and 1718; representative government; *export* salt, sponges, fruit, and dyewood. The **Leeward Islands** were grouped into a federation in 1871, with a representative government. They include :—Antigua, colonised by English, 1631, and Barbuda subject to it; Montserrat, colonised 1632, by English and French; St. Kitts, ceded by France in 1713, with Anguilla subject to it, colonised by English in 1650; Dominica, ceded by France in 1783; and the Virgin Islands, settled by English from Anguilla in 1680. The chief *product* of the Leeward Islands is sugar, but coffee, indigo, cochineal, lime-juice, etc., are exported. The **Windward Islands**, which were also federated in 1871, include :—Barbadoes, the first island, claimed by the English, and colonised in 1625; Grenada and the Grenadive Islands, taken from the French in 1763; St. Lucia, taken from the French in 1803; and St. Vincent, taken from the French in 1783. They all have a representative government. Chief *exports*, sugar, coffee, timber, fruits. Barbadoes is the most prosperous. **Jamaica**, captured from Spain in 1655, has a representative government; large and fertile; principal *products* are sugar, rum, coffee, spices, ginger, cocoa, tobacco, logwood, while timber is plentiful, and lead and other metals are found. The **Turks** and **Caicos Islands** are subject to Jamaica. **Trinidad** was also taken from Spain in 1797, and is a Crown colony; a large and fertile island; *exports* sugar, coffee, timber, cocoa-nuts, fruits, and pitch from a pitch lake. **Tobago**, finally taken from the French in 1803; is now annexed to Trinidad, *exports* sugar, molasses, rum, and fruits.

§ 97. In the SOUTH ATLANTIC England possesses several islands, none of much importance, except as naval stations. They are :— **Ascension Island**, occupied in 1815; a naval station with only 140 inhabitants. **St. Helena**, taken from the Dutch in 1673; a victualling place for ships; under a governor. **Tristan d'Acunha**, occupied in 1815, has only 90 people, who keep sheep and cattle, and grow vegetables for ships. The **Trinidad Islands**, occupied in 1815, are rarely visited. The **Falkland Islands** were annexed in 1833; Crown colony; *export* frozen meat, rear sheep and cattle, and are useful as a victualling place for ships. **South Georgia** is an island subject to the Governor of the Falkland Islands, but is barren.

§ 98. AFRICA.—On this continent England has very large and extensive possessions, chiefly south of the equator. **Cape Colony**, taken from the Dutch, 1806, was settled in 1820 by a body of 4,000 English emigrants; responsible government (1872); Kaffraria was incorporated 1865; Basutoland, annexed in 1868-71; West Griqualand, ceded in 1871; Griqualand, East Transkei, and Pembuland have been annexed to Cape Colony since 1876; Pondoland, Bechuanaland, are protectorates; *exports* wool, mohair, hides, skins, ivory, ostrich feathers, diamonds, gold, copper, wine, aloes, and grain. **Rhodesia** is under a chartered Company. **Natal** was settled by English and Dutch, in 1835, from Cape Colony; it became a separate colony, 1856; representative government; its products are similar to those of Cape Colony, and sugar, coffee, maize, and tropical fruits are grown. **Zululand** is a dependency of Natal since the war of 1879. On the West Coast we have some settlements that are more of the nature of "factories" than colonies. They are:—**Sierra Leone**, colony for freed slaves, established 1787, and made a Crown colony, 1808; *products*, coffee, rice, maize, ginger, pepper, and arrowroot. **British Sherbro** was added to it in 1862; it *exports* palm oil and salt. **Gambia** consists of settlements at the mouth of River Gambia, with stations in the interior; founded 1588 for trading purposes; now under Governor of Sierra Leone; it *exports* wax, ivory, gold dust, palm oil, rice, timber, and nuts. **Gold Coast Colony**, gained by purchase since 1661; Crown colony; trading settlement; *exports* gold, palm oil, ivory, caoutchouc, etc. **Lagos**, formed into colony in 1861; has a fine harbour, the Liverpool of West Africa; subordinate to Governor of Gold Coast; *exports* palm oil and kernels, pepper, grain, nuts, cotton, silk, and indigo. England also holds the **Slave Coast**, and the protectorate of the **Niger Districts** since 1884; the territories at the mouth of the River Niger have been acquired for us by the Royal Niger Company, which trades there. Trade same as Lagos. In East Africa we have the **Somali Coast**, a protectorate dependent on Aden; *exports* sheep and cattle. **Zanzibar Island**, acquired 1890, protectorate; *exports* ivory, caoutchouc, sesame seeds, cloves. **British East Africa**, which, till 1895, was the territory of the British East African Company, extends from the coast at Mombasa to the Lake Victoria Nyanza; that of the **African Lakes Company** from the River Zambesi to the south end of Lake Tanganyika. These territories are now being opened up for trade, and are said to be fertile. The **British South African Company** is developing Rhodesia, the country south of the Zambesi, including Mashonaland, a fertile country where gold is found. The possessions of these companies may become very important in the future.

The total area of all of our colonies throughout our empire is some 9,000,000 square miles, with a population of 290,000,000.

§ 99. *Concluding note.*[1] It is sometimes asked, **of what advantage** are our colonies to Great Britain? We might answer that the advantages are :—(1) Commercial, in exchanging their raw produce for British manufactures, in affording useful scope for the employment of British capital, and in promoting trade generally; (2) social, by affording fields for emigration and by the general diffusion of the British race; (3) political, by increasing the resources and prestige of Great Britain. The advantages secured by the colonies are a good system of government, protection in case of need, a market in Great Britain for their products, and the use of British capital and labour for developing their own resources.

[1] From Baker's *Geography of the British Empire*, p. 12.

NOTE ON AUTHORITIES.

BESIDES the books quoted in the footnotes to the text, the following will be found useful for reference and for further reading. The list is extracted from Professor C. F. Bastable's article on "British Commerce" in the *Dictionary of Political Economy:*—

"Anderson, *Historical and Chronological Deduction of the Origin of Commerce*, London, 1764.—Macpherson, *Annals of Commerce*, London, 1805, which is based on Anderson for the period 1492 to 1760, but the earlier part and the conclusion to 1800 by Macpherson solely. —G. L. Craik, *The History of British Commerce*, London, 1844; compiled from the preceding.—W. S. Lindsay, *History of Merchant Shipping and Ancient Commerce*, London, 1874-76, with notices of commerce in the first two volumes.—W. Cunningham, *Growth of English Industry and Commerce*, in two volumes, Cambridge, 1890 and 1892 [of which the second volume deals with modern times since Elizabeth].—Thorold Rogers, *History of Agriculture and Prices*, 6 vols., Oxford, 1866-88, devotes special chapters to foreign trade (vol. I., ch. 8; vol. IV., ch. 4; vol. V., ch. 5.)—[The same author's lectures on *The Economic Interpretation of History*, London, 1888, are most valuable and interesting].—Leone Levi, *History of British Commerce*, 1763-1878, London, 1880, has collected evidence on the growth of commerce in the 18th century.—Hubert Hall, *A History of the Custom Revenue of England*, 1885, illustrates the course and methods of the mediæval trade of England.—H. de B. Gibbins, *History of Commerce in Europe*, London, 1891 (bk. ii., ch. 7; bk. iii., chs. 3 and 6), and *Industrial History of England*, 2nd edition, London, 1891, gives a good brief account of the growth of foreign trade. For legislation, charters, and diplomatic documents, the sources are: *The Statutes of the Realm*, London, 1810-22, and Rymer, *Fœdera*, London, 1704-1717. Also cf. *Industry in England* (London, 1896), by H. de B. Gibbins.

For British Colonies, see C. P. Lucas' *Historical Geography of the British Colonies;* the *Colonial Office List*, published every year; Sir R. Rawson's *Tariffs and Trade of the British Empire*, 1888, and *Sequel*, 1889; Payne's *European Colonies;* Caldecott's *English Colonisation and Empire;* Seeley's *Expansion of England;* and Sir C. Dilke's *Problems of Greater Britain.*

TABLE OF SOME IMPORTANT DATES.

	YEAR.	PAGE.
Accession of Queen Elizabeth	1558	
Queen Elizabeth's alliance with Holland . .	1579	4
Drake's voyage round the world . . .	1577-80	4
Sack of Antwerp by Spanish army . . .	1585	12
Charter granted to East India Company . .	1600	7
James I.	1603	
Settlement of Virginia	1607	20
(For other colonies, see list, p. 23).		
John Bate's case	1606	27
Book of Rates issued	1608	2\
First factory of East India Company founded at		16
Surat	1612	
Abolition of monopolies	1624	16
Charles I.	1625	
Tunnage and poundage question . . .	1625-41	29
Ship money (first writ)	1634	30
Commonwealth proclaimed	1649	
General Post established	1656	34
Charles II.	1660	
The Stop of the Exchequer	1672	37
Navigation Acts	1651	38
James II.	1685	
Revocation of Edict of Nantes	1685	41
William and Mary	1689	
Bank of England founded	1693	44
Restoration of the Currency	1696	47
Treaty of Ryswick	1697	47
The Darien colony	1698	56
New East India Company	1698	67
The Methuen Treaty	1703	53
Anne	1702	
Union between England and Scotland . .	1707	55
New and Old East India Companies united .	1708	67

TABLE OF DATES.

	YEAR.	PAGE.
War of Spanish succession	1702-13	58
Treaty of Utrecht	1713	58
George I.	1714	
South Sea Bubble collapsed	1721	62
George II.	1727	
War of Austrian succession	1741-48	64
Peace of Aix-la-Chapelle	1748	68
Clive's capture of Arcot	1751	70
Seven Years' war	1756-63	64
Treaty of Paris	1763	85
Battle of Plassey	1757	71
Conquest of Canada	1759-60	85
George III.	1760	
Battle of Wandewash	1760	71
Pondicherry taken from French	1761	71
The Bridgewater Canal cut	1761	91
Battle of Buxar	1764	72
Stamp Act in American colonies	1765	86
Watt patented a steam-engine	1769	89
Hargreaves patented the spinning-jenny	1770	89
North's India " Regulating Act "	1773	74
Warren Hastings Governor of India	1772-85	74
Declaration of American Independence	1776	87
Crompton invented the "mule"	1779	89
Fox's India Bill	1783	75
Pitt's India Bill	1784	75
Rodney's naval victory (West Indies)	1782	119
Peace with American States	1782	87
Treaty of Versailles	1783	
Crompton patented the power-loom	1785	90
The Eden treaty with France	1786	93
Port Jackson settlement in Australia	1788	120
Beginning of the great Continental war (chiefly against France)	1793	93
William Pitt (the younger premier)	1783 / 1800 / 1804-06	
Bank of England suspended cash payments	1797	98
Union with Ireland	1801	100
Napoleon's Berlin decree	1806	95
Cape of Good Hope occupied	1806	119
Napoleon's Milan decree	1807	95
Conclusion of War by Peace of Paris	1815	
George IV.	1820	
Beginnings of Free Trade	1821	102

TABLE OF DATES.

	YEAR.	PAGE.
Resumption of cash payments	1821	110
Stockton and Darlington Railway opened	1825	106
William IV.	**1830**	
Queen Victoria.	**1837**	
Telegraph patented	1837	106
Steamer passages to America	1838	106
New Zealand occupied	1840	121
Penny Post established	1840	106
First Chinese war	1840	116
Repeal of the Corn Laws	1846-49	105
Repeal of the Navigation Acts	1849	105
Discovery of gold in Australia	1851	121
Second Chinese war	1856	116
The Indian Mutiny	1857	77
The "Canadian Dominion" formed	1867	123
Discovery of diamonds in South Africa	1867	124
Suez Canal opened	1869	117
England acquires Cyprus	1878	117
Dual control of Egypt by France and England	1879	117
Egyptian wars (Arabi Pasha and Mahdi)	1882-83	117
Discovery of gold in the Transvaal	1886	
Occupation of Mashonaland and Matabeleland	1889-94	133

INDEX.

N.B.—The numbers refer to the sections, not to the pages.

A
Africa, trade with, 9
African colonies, 70, 88
America, South, trade with, 70, 77, 80
America, North, trade with, 57, 77, 78
American colonies, 57-62
———— ———— war with, 62
Australian colonies, 70, 77, 86

B
Bank of England, 33, 71, 79
Banking, 28
Bate's Case, 21
Board of Trade, 36
Book of Rates, the, 21
Bullion, export of, 2

C
Canada, 59, 87
Canals, 65
Cape, the, 70, 88
Cavendish, Thomas, 5
Charles I. and revenue, 23
China, 82
Civil War, 28
Clive, 48-50
Coal trade, 81
Cobden, 75
Colonial trade, 29, 81
Colonisation and colonies, 17-20, 70, 84-99, and see names of countries in Appendix I.

Companies, various trading, 6-9
———— for colonisation, 18
Corn Laws, 2, 37, 75
Cotton trade, 77, 80
Crises, commercial, 77
Currency, restoration of, 13, 35

D
Darien scheme, 40
Davis, John, 5
Domestic system of industry, the, 63
Drake, Sir Francis, 5
Dupleix, 47

E
East India Company, the, 8, 9, 25, 44-56
Eden Treaty, the, 67*n*.
Egypt, 83
Empire, the British, survey of, 90-99
Enumerated articles, the, 58
Exchequer, stop of the, 28
Export trade, 38, 67, 70, 81

F
Factories abroad, 20; in India, 44
Fisheries, 16
Flemish weavers in England, 12
Fox's India Bill, 52
Frobisher, Martin, 5
France, the great war with (1793 to 1815), 67-71
Free trade, policy of, 74

139

INDEX.

G
Gold in Australia, 77, 86
—— in Africa, 88
Goldsmiths and banking, 28
Growth of English commerce, 10, 11, 19, 25, 31, 67, 73

H
Hansa, the, and England, 12
Hastings, Warren, 51
Hawkins, Sir John, 5
Hong Kong, 89
Huguenots in England, 32
Huskisson, 74

I
India, 7, 44-56, 92
—— attempts to reach, 7
—— development of, 55; modern trade of, 56
—— cotton factories in, 81
Inventions, the great, 64
Ireland and Irish commerce, 72
—— and England, union of, 72
—— potato famine in, 75n
—— Bank of, 79n
Iron trade, 81

J
"Jenkin's ear," War of, 43

L
Land tax, 34
Levant Company, the, 6, 7, 25
London, growth of, 26
Louis XIV., 41

M
M'Kinley Tariff, the, 78
Mercantile System, the, 2
Methuen Treaty, 39
Mining, 65
Monopolies and the Monopoly System, 14, 15

N
Napoleon's decrees, 69
National Debt, the, 33, 71
Navigation Acts, 30, 74

North-West passage, 5n.

P
Paris, Treaty of, 60
Peel, 75, 79
Pitt, 43; his India Bill, 52; his finance, 71
Plantations, 20
Policy, English commercial, 58, 74
Post, the, 26

R
Railways, 76
Recent growth of English commerce, 1
Revolution of 1688, the, 33
—— the Industrial, 63-66
Royal Exchange, 13
Ryswick, Treaty of, 35

S
Scotland and England, union of, 40, 58
Scotland, Bank of, 79
Shipping, 2, 16, 38
Ship Money, 24
Singapore, 89
South Sea Bubble, 42
—— trade, 43
Spain and England, 4, 43
Steam, use of, 64
Steamships, 76
Suez Canal, 56, 76, 83

T
Tunnage and Poundage, 22

U
Utrecht, Treaty of, 41

W
Walpole, 43
Wealth, distribution of, (17th century), 27
West Indian colonies, 20, 70, 80, 85, 97
Wool and woollen trade, 11, 16, 37, 80, 81

A LIST OF SCHOOL BOOKS
COMPILED AND EDITED BY
A. M. M. STEDMAN M.A.
WADHAM COLLEGE
OXON.

CONTENTS

	PAGE
INITIA LATINA	2
FIRST LATIN LESSONS	2
A FIRST LATIN READER	4
EASY SELECTIONS FROM CAESAR AND LIVY	4
EASY LATIN PASSAGES FOR UNSEEN TRANSLATION	6
EXEMPLA LATINA	8
EASY LATIN EXERCISES	8
THE LATIN COMPOUND SENTENCE	10
NOTANDA QUÆDAM	12
LATIN VOCABULARIES FOR REPETITION	14
LATIN EXAMINATION PAPERS, AND KEY	16
A SHORTER GREEK PRIMER	18
EASY GREEK PASSAGES FOR UNSEEN TRANSLATION	18
FIRST GREEK LESSONS	18
EASY GREEK EXERCISES ON ELEMENTARY SYNTAX	18
GREEK VOCABULARIES FOR REPETITION	18
GREEK TESTAMENT SELECTIONS	20
GREEK EXAMINATION PAPERS, AND KEY	22
FIRST FRENCH LESSONS	24
EASY FRENCH PASSAGES FOR UNSEEN TRANSLATION	24
EASY FRENCH EXERCISES ON ELEMENTARY SYNTAX	24
FRENCH VOCABULARIES FOR REPETITION	24
FRENCH EXAMINATION PAPERS, AND KEY	26
GENERAL KNOWLEDGE EXAMINATION PAPERS, AND KEY	28
CLASSICAL TRANSLATIONS	30
METHUEN'S COMMERCIAL SERIES	30
NEW SCHOOL BOOKS	31
SCHOOL EXAMINATION SERIES	32

METHUEN & CO., 36, ESSEX STREET, W.C.
G. BELL & SONS, YORK STREET, W.C.

March 1899.

Third Edition. Fcap. 8vo. 1s.

INITIA LATINA

EASY LESSONS ON ELEMENTARY ACCIDENCE

"The book is very easy and well suited to little boys."—*Journal of Education.*

"This will be found a useful book, for it carries out the injunction, so necessary for successful teaching, 'line upon line, precept upon precept.'"—*Spectator.*

Fifth Edition. Crown 8vo. 2s.

FIRST LATIN LESSONS

This book is much fuller than *Initia Latina*, and while it is not less simple, it will carry a boy a good deal further in the study of elementary Latin. The Exercises are more numerous, some easy translation adapted from Caesar has been added, and a few easy Examination Papers will afford a useful test of a boy's knowledge of his grammar. The book is intended to form a companion book to the *Shorter Latin Primer.*

Uniform with above.

FIRST FRENCH LESSONS. *Third Edition. Crown 8vo. 1s.*

[Specimen Page.]
Initia Latina.

I. Show which of the following Verbs are Transitive, and which are Intransitive—
The girl stands. The boys love the mother. The dog runs. The master teaches the boy. The girl sings. The queen praises the boy. Nauta stat. Puer canit. Puer Juliam amat. Julia currit.

II. Point out the Subject, Object, and Predicate in each of the following, writing the proper letters over each word—
The queen loves the boy. The boy fears the dog. The slave loves the girl. Puella servum timet. Servus canem terret. Homo reginam amat.

III. Translate into English—
1. Servus stat. 2. Servus cănem tĭmet. 3. Hŏmo currit. 4. Cănis hŏmĭnem terret. 5. Puella cănem ămat. 6. Aqua currit. 7. Puer puellam dŏcet. 8. Măgister servum dŏcet. 9. Servus nautam vĭdet. 10. Cănis puellam terret. 11. Hŏmo servum vĭdet. 12. Puella cănit. 13. Păter matrem ămat. 14. Māter filium dŏcet. 15. Nauta pugnat.

IV. Translate into Latin—
1. The slave runs. 2. The queen sees the slave. 3. The girl sees the sailor. 4. The man stands. 5. The water runs. 6. The boy sings. 7. The girl sees the water. 8. Caesar rules the land.

Fourth Edition, Revised. 18mo. 1s. 6d.

A FIRST LATIN READER

WITH NOTES ADAPTED TO SHORTER LATIN PRIMER, AND VOCABULARY

A collection of easy passages without difficulties of construction or thought. The book commences with simple sentences and passes on to connected passages, including the history of Rome and the invasion of Britain, simplified from Eutropius and Caesar.

Second Edition. 18mo. 1s.

EASY SELECTIONS FROM CAESAR

PART I.
THE HELVETIAN WAR.

WITH NOTES ADAPTED TO SHORTER LATIN PRIMER AND VOCABULARY.

18mo. 1s. 6d.

EASY SELECTIONS FROM LIVY

WITH INTRODUCTION, NOTES, VOCABULARY, MAPS, AND ILLUSTRATIONS.

THE SEVEN KINGS OF ROME.

[4]

[Specimen Page.]

FIRST LATIN READER.

est. Helvetii nostrorum impetus diutius sustinere non poterant. alteri in montem se receperunt: alteri ad impedimenta et carros suos se contulerunt. ab hora septima ad vesperum pugnatum est, nec hoc toto proelio aversum hostem videre quisquam potuit.

297. Dum vires annique sinunt, tolerate labores:
jam veniet tacito curva senecta pede.

298. Darius in fuga, cum aquam turbidam et cadaveribus inquinatam bibisset, negavit unquam se bibisse jucundius. nunquam videlicet sitiens biberat.

299. Quid magis est durum saxo, quid mollius unda!
dura tamen molli saxa cavantur aqua.

300. Catilina a Cicerone consule urbe expulsus est, et socii ejus deprehensi in carcere strangulati sunt.

301. Tempori cedere, id est necessitati parere, semper sapientis est habitum.

302. Fame coacta vulpes alta in vinea
uvam appetebat, summis saliens viribus:
quam tangere ut non potuit, discedens ait:
nondum matura est, nolo acerbam sumere.

303. Seneca haec ad amicum scripsit: Ante senectutem curavi, ut bene viverem; in senectute curo, ut bene e vita decedam.

304. Si Alexander, qui tot gentes armis devicit, etiam animi sui cupiditates vicisset, diutius haud dubie et majore cum gloria vixisset.

305. Praeceptores erudiunt pueros, servi dominis serviunt, cives legibus obediunt.

Sixth Edition, revised and enlarged.

Fcap. 8vo. 1s. 6d.

EASY LATIN PASSAGES
FOR
UNSEEN TRANSLATION

The attention which is now rightly given to unprepared translation necessitates early practice. There are many excellent manuals, but most of these are too hard for beginners, for whose use the above volume has been compiled. The pieces are graduated in length and difficulty, and the early pieces present no serious obstacles.

"The selections are carefully chosen and judiciously graduated, and seem very well adapted to the needs of schoolboys."—*Private Schoolmaster.*

Uniform with above.

EASY GREEK PASSAGES.   *Third Edition, Revised.*
Fcap. 8vo. 1s. 6d.

EASY FRENCH PASSAGES.   *Third Edition, Revised.*
Fcap. 8vo. 1s. 6d.

[Specimen Page.]

EASY LATIN PASSAGES.

TITUS.

321. Titus amor ac deliciae generis humani appellatus est. admonentibus domesticis, quia plura polliceretur, quam praestare posset, non oportere, ait, quemquam a sermone principis tristem discedere. atque etiam recordatus quondam super coenam, quod nihil cuiquam toto die praestitisset, memorabilem illam meritoque laudatam vocem edidit : Amici, diem perdidi !

THE LIMITS OF PLAY.

322. Lusus pueris proderunt; quia pueri post lusus plus virium et acriorem animum afferunt ad discendum. modus tamen sit remissionibus; ne aut negatae odium studiorum faciant, aut nimiae otii consuetudinem afferant.

323.   AN OLD HALL.

Quin etiam veterum effigies ex ordine avorum
antiqua e cedro, Italusque paterque Sabinus
vitisator, curvam servans sub imagine falcem,
Saturnusque senex Janique bifrontis imago
vestibulo adstabant, aliique ab origine reges,
martiaque ob patriam pugnando vulnera passi;
multaque praeterea sacris in postibus arma,
captivi pendent currus curvaeque secures,
et cristae capitum et portarum ingentia claustra,
spiculaque clipeique ereptaque rostra carinis.

AN "ADMIRABLE CRICHTON."

324. Eleus Hippias, cum Olympiam venisset, gloriatus est, cuncta paene audiente Graecia, nihil esse ulla in arte rerum omnium, quod ipse nesciret; nec solum has artes, quibus liberales doctrinae atque ingenuae continerentur, geometriam, musicam, litterarum cognitionem et poëtarum, atque illa, quae de naturis rerum, quae de hominum moribus, quae de rebuspublicis dicerentur : sed anulum, quem haberet, pallium, quo amictus, soccos, quibus indutus esset, se sua manu confecisse.

Crown 8vo. 1s.

EXEMPLA LATINA

FIRST EXERCISES ON LATIN ACCIDENCE

WITH VOCABULARY

This book is intended to be used midway between a book of elementary lessons and more difficult Exercises on Syntax. It contains simple and copious exercises on Accidence and elementary Syntax. Each Exercise has two parts (A, B).

ISSUED WITH THE CONSENT OF DR. KENNEDY.

Seventh and Cheaper Edition, Revised. Crown 8vo. 1s. 6d.

EASY LATIN EXERCISES

ON THE SYNTAX OF THE
REVISED AND SHORTER LATIN PRIMERS

WITH VOCABULARY

This book has been compiled to accompany DR. KENNEDY'S 'Shorter Latin Primer' and 'Revised Latin Primer.' Special attention has been paid to the rules of *oratio obliqua*, and the exercises are numerous. DR. KENNEDY has kindly allowed his Syntax rules to be incorporated in the book.

The 2s. 6d. edition of this book may still be obtained.

EASY FRENCH EXERCISES. *Crown 8vo. 2s. 6d.*

THE ABLATIVE CASE.

The Ablative is the Case which defines circumstances; it is rendered by many prepositions, *from, with, by, in.*

Ablative of Separation.

The **Ablative of Separation** is used with Verbs meaning *to remove, release, deprive, want*; with Adjectives such as liber, *free*; also the Adverb procul, *far from* :

Populus Atheniensis Phocionem patriâ pepulit. NEP.
The Athenian people drove Phocion from his country.

The **Ablative of Origin** is used with Verbs, chiefly Participles, implying descent or origin :

Tantalo prognatus, Pelope natus.
Descended from Tantalus, son of Pelops.

18.

1. The death of Hannibal freed the Romans from fear.
2. No one is free from blame.
3. We are in need of brave soldiers.
4. They stripped the town of defenders.
5. The Helvetii did not abstain from wrong.
6. Caesar calls the soldiers away from the battle.
7. The praetors kept the crowd from the forum.
8. Tarquin, the last king of the Romans, was expelled from the city.
9. The murderers abandoned their attempt.
10. Hippocrates was descended from a Syracusan family.
11. Caesar cut off the enemy from their supplies.
12. He was descended from Hercules.
13. I will relieve you of this load.
14. Love of virtue ought to restrain us from wrong.
15. We hear that he is descended from an ancient family.

Crown 8vo. 1s. 6d.

WITH VOCABULARY, &c.

THE
LATIN COMPOUND SENTENCE
RULES AND EXERCISES

This book has been compiled to meet the requirements of boys who have worked through a book of easy exercises on Syntax and who need methodical teaching on the Compound Sentence. In the main the arrangement of the Revised Latin Primer has been followed, not without some doubts whether such arrangement is in all cases correct. But on the whole I have thought it best to suggest an alternative classification in the notes. Exercise on *oratio obliqua* are added.

Each Exercise has two parts (A, B).

[Specimen Page.]

LATIN COMPOUND SENTENCE.

8. Leave nothing undone[1] to avenge your brother.
9. It was[2] all through you that I did not defeat the enemy.
10. We shall not prevent them doing that.

III. Indirect Questions.

15. Clauses containing **Indirect Questions** have a verb in the conjunctive, and are joined by interrogative pronouns or conjunctions with the principal verb:

> Quæsivit *cur hæc fecissem.*
> *He inquired why I had done this.*

> Rogaverunt quando futurum esset ut pons conficeretur.
> *They asked when the bridge would be finished.*

Note 1.—The principal verb need not be of an interrogative character:

> Moneo *quid faciendum sit.*
> *I warn you what you ought to do.*

Note 2.—The conjunctions *if, whether,* must never be translated by *si, sive,* but by *-ne, num, nonne*:

> Dic mihi *num valeat.*
> *Tell me if he is well.*

Note 3.—For a future conjunctive passive the periphrastic forms *futurum sit, fuerit, esset* (followed by *ut* and conjunctive) must be used.

Note 4.—Nescio quis, nescio quomodo (*some one, somehow*) are treated as simple expressions and do not take the conjunctive:

> *Nescio quis* venit.
> *Some one came.*

---

[1] Prætermitto.   [2] Sbo.

Third Edition. Fcap. 8vo. 1s. 6d.
WITH VOCABULARY, 2s.

NOTANDA QUÆDAM:

MISCELLANEOUS LATIN EXERCISES

ON

COMMON RULES AND IDIOMS.

This volume is designed to supply miscellaneous practice in those rules and idioms with which boys are supposed to be familiar. Each exercise consists of ten miscellaneous sentences, and the exercises are carefully graduated. The book may be used side by side with the manuals in regular use. It will probably be found very useful by pupils preparing for Public Schools, Local, Army, and minor University examinations.

[12]

Notanda Quaedam.

4. Caius swore that he would never do anything that was unworthy of a Roman citizen.
5. The river was so rapid that the army could not cross without great danger.
6. The boy asked me whether the old man had lived all his life at Gades.
7. He advised us to be mindful of the shortness of life.
8. He has been made heir to the whole estate.
9. I hope the poor citizens will be spared.
10. You are weak compared to him.

LXVIII.

1. The Senate was nearly all on the side of Hannibal.
2. The dictator swore that if no one followed he would die alone for his country.
3. He ordered the centurion not to kill the prisoners.
4. Who is there that does not love the old generals of Rome?
5. He gave the soldiers two pounds of corn apiece.

Seventh Edition, revised. Fcap. 8vo. 1s. 6d.

LATIN VOCABULARIES
FOR REPETITION:
ARRANGED ACCORDING TO SUBJECTS.

In this book an attempt has been made to remedy that scantiness of vocabulary which characterizes most boys. The words are arranged according to subjects in vocabularies of twelve words each, and if the matter of this little book of eighty-nine pages is committed to memory, the pupil will have a good stock of words on every subject. The idea has received the sanction of many eminent authorities.

"This little book will be found very valuable by those studying Latin, and especially by those preparing for scholarship exams. at the Public Schools."—*Practical Teacher.*

"A most ingenious idea, and quite worthy of a trial."—*The Head Master of Eton.*

"A book likely to prove most useful. I have been all through it with care, and can testify to its accuracy."—*The Head Master of Charterhouse.*

Uniform with above.

GREEK VOCABULARIES *Second Edition.* Fcap. 8vo. 1s. 6d.
FRENCH VOCABULARIES *Sixth Edition.* Fcap. 8vo. 1s.

[Specimen Page.]

WAR.

ĕquĭtātus,	-ūs,	*cavalry.*
pĕdĭtātus,	-ūs,	*infantry.*
mănus,	-ūs,	*band.*
trĭpertīto,		*in three divisions.*
quam maxĭmus,	-ī -ae -ĭ,	*as great as possible.*
hăbeo,	(2),	*hold (levy).*
convĕnĭo,	-vēnī -ventum,	*assemble.*
conscrībo,	-psī -ptum,	*enrol.*
compăro,	(1),	*raise.*
cōgo,	coēgī, coactum,	*collect, compel.*

39. [xxxvi.] *War (Service).*

stīpendium,	-iī,	*pay, service, tribute.*
missio,	-ōnis,	*discharge.*
mīlĭtĭa,	-ae,	*warfare, military service.*
sācrāmentum,	-ī,	*oath.*
tīro,	-ōnis,	*recruit.*
vĕtĕrānus,	-ī,	*veteran.*
immūnĭtas,	-ātis,	*exemption.*
ēmĕrĭtī,	-ōrum	*soldiers who have served their time.*
vexillārĭī,	-ōrum,	*reserve forces.*
in verba jūro,	(1),	*swear (according to a formulary).*
mĕreor,	-ĭtus,	*serve, deserve.*
mīlĭto,	(1),	*serve (as a soldier).*

40. [xxxvii.] *War (Camp).*

tăbernācŭlum,	-ī,	*tent.*
praetōrium,	-iī,	*general's tent.*
porta dĕcŭmāna,	-ae -ae,	*main gate of camp.*
castra hīberna,	-ōrum,	*winter camp.*
castra aestīva,	-ōrum,	*summer camp.*
castra stătīva,	-ōrum,	*stationary camp.*
ăpertus,	-ī -ae -ĭ,	*open, unprotected.*

c

Crown 8vo. 2s. 6d.
Ninth Edition, Revised.

LATIN EXAMINATION PAPERS
IN MISCELLANEOUS GRAMMAR AND IDIOMS.

"A most useful and learned book."—*Professor Kennedy.*

"This useful collection of papers, which are graduated in difficulty, is well adapted 'to provide boys who have passed beyond the elementary stages of grammar and scholarship with practice in miscellaneous grammar and idioms.' The work seems to be better than most compilations of this kind."—*Athenæum.*

"The book is practical and cheap, and the questions are clearly worded. None of the ordinary rules or anomalies escape attention. Mr. Stedman says quite truly that 'the papers are graduated in difficulty.' Those at the beginning would suit ordinary Fourth and Fifth Forms or candidates for Woolwich and Sandhurst; and the later sets of questions would give useful practice to boys working for University scholarships."—*Saturday Review.*

A KEY TO THE ABOVE, by P. HEBBLETHWAITE, M.A. Issued to Tutors on application to the Publishers. *Third Edition.* Price 6s. net.

Second Edition, Re-written. 18mo. 1s.

A VOCABULARY OF LATIN IDIOMS AND PHRASES

[16]

[Specimen Page.]

Latin Examination Papers.

2. What is the difference in meaning between the singular and plural of—comitium, littera, ludus, tabula?

3. Translate—what does it matter to me? accused of embezzlement; a house of marble; the day after the battle; after the rising of the sun; do not lie; more than three months; to Naples; lighter than gold; at least; at length.

4. Explain the forms—quî, sultis, viden, fervit.

5. Translate and comment on—(1) Opus est *properato*. (2) *Parcite procedere*. (3) Non recusavit *quominus* poenam *subiret*. (4) Nullum intermisi diem *quin scriberem*.

6. Turn into *oratio recta*—(1) Dixit eum si hoc diceret, errare. (2) Dixit eum si hoc diceret, erraturum esse. (3) Dixit eum si hoc dixisset, erraturum fuisse.

7. Explain the figures in—(1) Pateris libamus et auro. (2) Insaniens sapientia. (3) Superbos Tarquini fasces. (4) Scuta latentia condunt. (5) Dulce loquens Lalage.

8. Give the constructions with—polliceor, impero, refert, vereor, quum, nē. Distinguish between the transitive and intransitive uses of—fugio, consulo, convenio.

9. What do you mean by—cardinal numbers, consecutive clause, co-ordinate sentence, diaeresis, enclitics, labials?

10. What English words are derived from—templum, metior, sidus, dexter, ambio? What were the original names of the months *Iulius* and *Augustus*?

11. Give an example of *coepi* in passive construction.

12. Translate—I know no one to trust. Do not prevent me from going. Do you know how many years Caesar lived? Who has seen the Pyramids without wondering at them? We are permitted to do this.

Crown 8vo. 1s. 6d.

A SHORTER GREEK PRIMER

This book contains the elements of Greek Accidence and Syntax in a compass of less than 100 pages.

Third Edition, Revised. Fcap. 8vo. 1s. 6d.

EASY GREEK PASSAGES FOR UNSEEN TRANSLATION

STEPS TO GREEK.
18*mo.* 1s.

EASY GREEK EXERCISES ON ELEMENTARY SYNTAX

In preparation.

Ready, Fcap. 8vo. 1s. 6d.
Second Edition.

GREEK VOCABULARIES FOR REPETITION:
ARRANGED ACCORDING TO SUBJECTS

The above books have been compiled in response to requests by teachers for companion volumes to the author's Latin books. They are constructed on the same principle.

[18]

[Specimen page.]

SHORTER GREEK PRIMER

Stems in o pure

Stem		Masc. φιλιο	Fem. φιλια	Neut. φιλιο
Singular	N.	φίλιος	φιλίᾱ	φίλιον
	V.	φίλιε	φιλίᾱ	φίλιον
	A.	φίλιον	φιλίᾱν	φίλιον
	G.	φιλίου	φιλίᾱς	φιλίου
	D.	φιλίῳ	φιλίᾳ	φιλίῳ
Dual	N.V.A.	φιλίω	φιλίω	φιλίω
	G.D.	φιλίοιν	φιλίοιν	φιλίοιν
Plural	N.V.	φίλιοι	φίλιαι	φίλια
	A.	φιλίους	φιλίας	φίλια
	G.	φιλίων	φιλίων	φιλίων
	D.	φιλίοις	φιλίαις	φιλίοις

Decline also: δίκαιος, *just;* ὅσιος, *holy.*

Contracted Adjectives

Stem		Masc. χρυσεο	Fem. χρυσεα	Neut. χρυσεο
Singular	N.	χρῡσοῦς	χρῡσῆ	χρῡσοῦν
	V.	χρῡσοῦς	χρῡσῆ	χρῡσοῦν
	A.	χρῡσοῦν	χρῡσῆν	χρῡσοῦν
	G.	χρῡσοῦ	χρῡσῆς	χρῡσοῦ
	D.	χρῡσῷ	χρῡσῇ	χρῡσῷ
Dual	N.V.A.	χρῡσώ	χρῡσώ	χρῡσώ
	G.D.	χρῡσοῖν	χρῡσοῖν	χρῡσοῖν
Plural	N.V.	χρῡσοῖ	χρῡσαῖ	χρῡσᾶ
	A.	χρῡσοῦς	χρῡσᾶς	χρῡσᾶ
	G.	χρῡσῶν	χρῡσῶν	χρῡσῶν
	D.	χρῡσοῖς	χρῡσαῖς	χρῡσοῖς

Decline also: ἁπλοῦς, *simple;* ἀργυροῦς, *of silver.*

Note 1.—Adjectives in -ους *pure* (like ἀργυροῦς) keep the *a* all through the Feminine Singular.

Note 2.—The methods of contraction should be carefully noted (cf. p. 5).

Third Edition, re-written.

Fcap. 8vo. 2s. 6d.

GREEK TESTAMENT SELECTIONS
FOR THE USE OF SCHOOLS.

New Edition. With Introduction, Notes, and Vocabulary.

This small volume contains a selection of passages, each sufficient for a lesson, from the Gospels, forming a life of Christ. In schools where only a limited time can be given to the study of the Greek Testament, an opportunity is thus supplied for reading some of the most characteristic and interesting passages.

The Third Edition has been carefully revised, and the notes re-written.

"When the first edition of this useful book was published, we ventured to predict that it would be highly appreciated and widely used. Such has been the case. A new edition has been called for, and a much enlarged and improved edition has been issued."—*Journal of Education.*

"The notes are full of the most useful matter, and the vocabulary is complete."—*Educational News.*

NOTES. 79

53 ἀγαθῶν] [R. 113.]
54 ἀντελάβετο] lit. 'took by the hand,' *i.e.*
'helped.' [R. 112.]
55 καθώς...ἡμῶν] These words form a parenthesis; 'that He might remember mercy (*even as He spake unto our fathers*) toward Abraham and his seed for ever.'
αἰῶνα] Cf. § 121. 46.

48. 1 ἐγένετο...ἐξῆλθεν] ἐγένετο is a translation of a Hebrew formula of transition; the verb which follows is sometimes connected with καί, sometimes, as here, has no connecting particle.

ἐν ταῖς ἡμέραις ἐκείναις] *i.e.* at the time of or shortly after the Annunciation.

ἀπογράφεσθαι] Either passive, 'should be enrolled,' or middle, 'should enrol themselves.' The ἀπογραφή was a registration, generally for purposes of taxation. Every Roman subject was liable to a capitation tax.

πᾶσαν τὴν οἰκουμένην] sc. γῆν, 'all the habitable world,' *i.e.* the Roman Empire.

2 αὕτη...Κυρηνίου] 'this was the first enrolment made,' lit. 'this enrolment took place as the first.' Quirinius was Governor of Syria in A.D. 6, ten years after this time. St. Luke has therefore been charged with a grave error in assigning the enrolment to Quirinius. It is probable however that Quirinius was twice governor of Syria, once in B.C. 4, when he began the census, and once in A.D. 6, when he carried it to completion.

τῆς Συρίας] [R. 95.]

3 ἀπογράφεσθαι] Infinitive of purpose.

4 Βηθλεέμ] 'the house of bread.' Joseph might have got himself registered at Nazareth, but the Jewish practice seems to have been to go to one's native town. The birth of Christ

Crown 8vo. 2s. 6d.
Fifth Edition, revised and enlarged.

GREEK EXAMINATION PAPERS

IN MISCELLANEOUS GRAMMAR AND IDIOMS.

"Teachers will find these papers very useful."—*Spectator.*

"Very useful for Teachers."—*Saturday Review.*

A KEY TO THE ABOVE, by P. HEBBLETHWAITE, M.A. Issued to Tutors and Private Students on application to the Publishers. *Second Edition. Price 6s. net.*

[Specimen Page.]

Greek Examination Papers.

5. Translate and comment on—(1) ἀκούσας δὲ αὐτῶν τρυζόντων...τῶν οἰκιῶν ὑμῶν ἐπιπριαμένων. (2) οὐκ ἀνέξομαι ζῶσα. (3) οὔ σοι μὴ μεθέψομαί ποτε. (4) ᾔδει ἄξιος ἂν ὢν θανάτου. (5) γραφὴν ἐδίωκε. (6) ἀμείβειν χρύσεα χαλκείων. (7) πυραμὶς μείζων πατρός. (8) ὁ μάντις τοὺς λόγους ψευδεῖς λέγει.

6. What notion generally precedes the use of πρίν?

Give rules for the construction of final sentences in Greek, with examples.

7. Give the Greek of—mast; sail; anchor; stern; the school of Plato; some people; with impunity; as far as was in their power; may you be happy; skilful in speaking; it being lawful; more honest than rich; fairer than any before; too heavy for a boy; we must obey him; he did it unseen; don't talk.

8. Is there any connection or similarity between the case-endings of Latin and Greek?

9. Translate—
 1. He sent for his wife and her son.
 2. Do not go away till I come.
 3. Surely you do not say so?

LXVIII.

1. Give the Genitive and Gender of—γάλα—ἐλπίς—ἄνθος—πίναξ—κράτος—σάρξ—φέγγος—χρώς—γενειάς—χελιδών.

2. Give the chief tenses of—αἴρω—ἐπιτίθημι—ἐλαύνω—σβέννυμι—ἐμπίπτω—δάκνω.

STEPS TO FRENCH
Fourth Edition. 18mo. 8d.
One of the easiest French Elementary Books in existence.

FIRST FRENCH LESSONS
Third Edition, Revised. Crown 8vo. 1s.

EASY FRENCH PASSAGES FOR UNSEEN TRANSLATION
Third Edition, Revised. Fcap. 8vo. 1s. 6d.

EASY FRENCH EXERCISES ON ELEMENTARY SYNTAX
With Vocabulary. Second Edition. Crown 8vo. 2s. 6d. In use at Charterhouse. *Key, 3s. net.*

FRENCH VOCABULARIES FOR REPETITION: Arranged according to Subjects
Seventh Edition. Fcap. 8vo. 1s.

The above four books are constructed on the same principle as the corresponding Latin books.

[Specimen page.]

IRREGULAR VERBS 73

VERBS

MOST COMMON IRREGULAR VERBS :—

Future.	Conditional.	Present Conjunctive.	Imperf. Conjunctive.	Imperative
j'irai	j'irais	que j'aille	que j'allasse	
tu iras	tu irais	que tu ailles	que tu allasses	va
il ira	il irait	qu'il aille	qu'il allât	
nous irons	nous irions	que nous allions	que nous allassions	allons
vous irez	vous iriez	que vous alliez	que vous allassiez	allez
ils iront	ils iraient	qu'ils aillent	qu'ils allassent	
je m'en irai	je m'en irais	que je m'en aille	que je m'en allasse	
tu t'en iras	tu t'en irais	que tu t'en ailles	que tu t'en allasses	va-t'en
il s'en ira (irons)	il s'en irait	qu'il s'en aille	qu'il s'en allât	
nous nous en	n. n. en irions	que n. n. en allions	que n. n. en allassions	allons-nous-
vous vous en irez	v. v. en iriez	que v. v. en alliez	que v. v. en allassiez	allez-vous-en
ils s'en iront	ils s'en iraient	qu'ils s'en aillent	qu'ils s'en allassent	
je battrai	je battrais	que je batte	que je battisse	
				bats
				battons
				battez
je boirai	je boirais	que je boive	que je busse	
tu boiras	tu boirais	que tu boives	que tu busses	bois
il boira	il boirait	qu'il boive	qu'il bût	
nous boirons	nous boirions	que nous buvions	que nous bussions	buvons
vous boirez	vous boiriez	que vous buviez	que vous bussiez	buvez
ils boiront	ils boiraient	qu'ils boivent	qu'ils bussent	
je connaîtrai	je connaîtrais	que je connaisse	que je connusse	
tu connaîtras	tu connaîtrais	que tu connaisses	que tu connusses	connais
il connaîtra	il connaîtrait	qu'il connaisse	qu'il connût	
nous connaîtrons	n. connaîtrions	que n. connaissions	que n. connussions	connaissons
vous connaîtrez	vous connaîtriez	que vous connaissiez	que vous connussiez	connaissez
ils connaîtront	ils connaîtraient	qu'ils connaissent	qu'ils connussent	
je courrai	je courrais	que je coure	que je courusse	
				cours
				courons
				courez
je croirai	je croirais	que je crois	que je crusse	
		que tu croies		crois
		qu'il croie		
		que nous croyions		croyons
		que vous croyiez		croyez
		qu'ils croient		

Ninth Edition. Crown 8vo. 2s. 6d.

FRENCH EXAMINATION PAPERS
IN MISCELLANEOUS GRAMMAR AND IDIOMS.

"I am delighted to find you have supplied a want in our School teaching, and produced a book which I have often wished to see started. I consider your Papers in their graduated arrangement are all that can be desired, and I shall strongly recommend them for use in the Modern Side and Army Class here."—*Rev. A. C. Clapin,* Sherborne, Examiner in French, Oxford and Cambridge Local Examinations.

"The book seems very well conceived, and likely to be of great service not only to boys entering the Public Schools, but to all those who are preparing for an examination. The idioms are remarkably well chosen."—*M. George Petilleau,* Charterhouse.

"I have used the French Examination Papers for some months with my private pupils, and I have found them very useful."—*M. Henri Bué,* Merchant Taylors.

"Your book is likely to prove very useful, and I have found it very suggestive."—*M. Eugène Fasnacht,* Westminster.

"No more convenient work could be written for teachers in Modern Classes. I have introduced it in my Upper Class."—*M. H. L. Guilmant,* Repton.

"I think your idea a very good one, and I shall take the first opportunity of making use of your book."—The *French Master,* Cheltenham.

A KEY TO THE ABOVE
Compiled by G. A. SCHRUMPF, B.A., Univ. of France

Issued to Tutors and Private Students only, on application to the Publishers. Fourth Edition. Price 6s. net.

[26]

[Specimen Page.]

LXXIII.

1. Compare—bon, mauvais, petit; and give the adverbs derived from these words. Translate—my best book is here; I am much better.

2. Distinguish—il me rit au nez, il rit de mon nez; excellent, excellant; différant, différent; le cours, la cour; le tour, la tour; vers, vert, le ver; faire grâce, faire une grâce; un écrivain malheureux, un malheureux écrivain.

3. What is the place of the adverb in a French sentence? Translate—I have slept well.

4. Give the masculine of—actrice, hôtesse, institutrice, bergère, jumelle, vache, de laquelle, joyeuse, grasses, sotte, citoyenne; and the plural of—joujou, nez, chacal, sous-officier.

5. What tenses are formed from the present participle? Give examples, and any exceptions you know.

6. Translate—
   1. I have passed you the salt.
   2. Have you left the door open?
   3. I have given your father the book I promised him.
   4. Who is there? It is he.
   5. I will give it him if you like.

7. Write the infinitive of—mis, sert, envoient, dû, fait, vu, ouvert.

8. Derive—agneau, aigu, ajouter, âme, arriver.

9. Why should the first person plural of *gémir* end in *-issons*, and that of *sentir* in *-ons*? What was the old form of *il aime*?

Crown 8vo. 2s. 6d.
Third Edition.

GENERAL KNOWLEDGE
EXAMINATION PAPERS.

These Papers have been compiled to furnish practice for those who are preparing for scholarships at the Public Schools and at the Universities. A large number of the Questions are original, a larger number taken from papers actually set. The first fifty papers are, on the whole, suitable for boys preparing for Public School Scholarships; the remainder for Candidates for the College Scholarships.

"They are sufficiently varied to suit boys of any age between twelve and eighteen."—*Guardian.*

"Great pains have been taken in the choice of subjects and in distinguishing what is technical from what is general."—*Educational Times.*

"Your General Knowledge Papers are splendid."—Head Master, Bolton Grammar School.

A KEY TO THE ABOVE.
Second Edition. Price 7s. net.

Issued to Tutors and Private Students only on application to the Publishers.

[28]

Classical Translations.

Edited by H. F. FOX, M.A., Fellow and Tutor of Brasenose College, Oxford.

Messrs. Methuen are issuing a New Series of Translations from the Greek and Latin Classics. They have enlisted the services of some of the best Oxford and Cambridge Scholars, and it is their intention that the Series shall be distinguished by literary excellence as well as by scholarly accuracy.

Crown 8vo.

CICERO—De Oratore I. Translated by E. N. P. MOOR, M.A., Assistant-Master at Clifton. 3s. 6d.

ÆSCHYLUS—Agamemnon, Chöephoroe, Eumenides. Translated by LEWIS CAMPBELL, LL.D., late Professor of Greek at St Andrews. 5s.

LUCIAN—Six Dialogues (Nigrinus, Icaro-Menippus, The Cock, The Ship, The Parasite, The Lover of Falsehood). Translated by S. T. IRWIN, M.A., Assistant-Master at Clifton; late Scholar of Exeter College, Oxford. 3s. 6d.

SOPHOCLES—Electra and Ajax. Translated by E. D. A. MORSHEAD, M.A., late Scholar of New College, Oxford; Assistant-Master at Winchester. 2s. 6d.

TACITUS—Agricola and Germania. Translated by R. B. TOWNSHEND, late Scholar of Trinity College, Cambridge. 2s. 6d.

CICERO—Select Orations (Pro Milone, Pro Murena, Philippic II., In Catilinam). Translated by H. E. D. BLAKISTON, M.A., Fellow and Tutor of Trinity College, Oxford. 5s.

CICERO—De Natura Deorum. Translated by F. BROOKS, M.A. 3s. 6d.

THE ODES AND EPODES OF HORACE. Translated by A. D. GODLEY, M.A., Fellow of Magdalen College, Oxford. 2s.

Methuen's Commercial Series.

Edited by H. DE B. GIBBINS, LITT.D., M.A.

Crown 8vo.

BRITISH COMMERCE AND COLONIES FROM ELIZABETH TO VICTORIA. By H. DE B. GIBBINS, LITT.D., M.A. *Third Edition.* 2s.

A FRENCH COMMERCIAL CORRESPONDENCE. By S. E. BALLY. *Second Edition.* 2s.

A FRENCH COMMERCIAL READER. By S. E. BALLY. 1s. 6d.

GERMAN COMMERCIAL CORRESPONDENCE. By S. E. BALLY. 2s. 6d.

COMMERCIAL GEOGRAPHY. With special reference to the British Empire. By L. D. LYDE, M.A. *Second Edition.* 2s.

COMMERCIAL EXAMINATION PAPERS. By H. DE B. GIBBINS, D.LITT., M.A. 1s. 6d.

Methuen's Commercial Series—*continued.*

THE ECONOMICS OF COMMERCE. By H. DE B. GIBBINS, LITT.D., M.A. 1s. 6d.

A PRIMER OF BUSINESS. By S. JACKSON, M.A. *Second Edition.* 1s. 6d.

COMMERCIAL ARITHMETIC. By F. G. TAYLOR, M.A. *Second Edition.* 1s. 6d.

PRÉCIS WRITING AND OFFICE CORRESPONDENCE. By E. E. WHITFIELD, M.A. 2s.

ESSENTIALS OF COMMERCIAL EDUCATION. By E. E. WHITFIELD, M.A. 1s. 6d.

AN ENTRANCE GUIDE TO PROFESSIONS AND BUSINESS. By HENRY JONES. 1s. 6d.

THE PRINCIPLES OF BOOK-KEEPING BY DOUBLE ENTRY. With Worked Examples and numerous Examination Papers. By J. E. B. M'ALLEN, M.A. (Lond.), Assistant-Master in the Liverpool College Middle School. 2s.

A GERMAN COMMERCIAL READER. By S. E. BALLY, Modern Language Master at the Manchester Grammar School.

A GEOGRAPHY OF THE CHIEF COMMERCIAL NATIONS: MORE ESPECIALLY OF ENGLAND'S COMPETITORS. By A. W. ANDREWS, M.A., F.R.G.S.

Text-Books of Technology.

Edited by Prof. W. GARNETT, D.C.L., Secretary of the Technical Education Board of the London County Council, and Prof. J. WERTHEIMER, B.Sc., B.A., F.I.C., F.C.S., Principal of the Merchant Venturers' Technical College, Bristol.

The following Volumes are published or in progress:—

1. HOW TO MAKE A DRESS. By Miss WOOD, Chief Instructress at the Goldsmith's Institute, New Cross. Crown 8vo, 1s. 6d. [*Ready.*

2. CARPENTRY AND JOINERY. By F. C. WEBBER, Chief Lecturer to the Building Trades' Department of the Merchant Venturers' Technical College, Bristol. Crown 8vo, 3s. 6d. [*Ready.*

3. PRACTICAL CHEMISTRY. By G. P. DARNELL-SMITH, B.Sc., A.I.C., F.C.S., Senior Lecturer in Chemistry at the Merchant Venturers' College.

4. DESIGNING AND WEAVING. By A. F. BARKER, Head Master of the Textile Department of the Bradford Technical College.

5. THE GEOLOGY OF COAL. By G. A. LEBOUR, M.A., F.G.S., Professor of Geology in the Durham College of Science, Newcastle-on-Tyne.

6. PRACTICAL MECHANICS. By S. H. WELLS, Principal of the Battersea Polytechnic Institute. [*Ready.*

7. PRACTICAL PHYSICS. By H. STROUD, D.Sc., M.A., Professor of Physics in the Durham College of Science, Newcastle-on-Tyne.

8. THE MANUFACTURE OF BOOTS. By E. SWAYSLAND, Technical Instructor, Northants County Council.

NEW SCHOOL BOOKS.

CLASSICAL.

TACITI AGRICOLA. With Introduction, Notes, Map, etc. By R. F. DAVIS, M.A., Assistant-Master at Weymouth College. Crown 8vo, 2s.

TACITI GERMANIA. By the same Editor. Crown 8vo, 2s.

DEMOSTHENES AGAINST CONON AND CALLICLES. Edited, with Notes and Vocabulary, by F. DARWIN SWIFT, M.A., formerly Scholar of Queen's College, Oxford; Assistant-Master at Denstone College. Fcap. 8vo, 2s.

PASSAGES FOR UNSEEN TRANSLATION. By E. C. MARCHANT, M.A., Fellow of Peterhouse, Cambridge, and A. M. COOK, M.A., late Scholar of Wadham College, Oxford, Assistant-Masters at St. Paul's School. Crown 8vo, 3s. 6d.

This book contains two hundred Latin and two hundred Greek Passages, and has been very carefully compiled to meet the wants of V. and VI. Form boys at Public Schools. It is also well adapted for the use of Honourmen at the Universities.

EXERCISES IN LATIN ACCIDENCE. By S. E. WINBOLT, Assistant-Master in Christ's Hospital. Crown 8vo, 1s. 6d.

An elementary book adapted for Lower Forms, to accompany the shorter Latin Primer.

NOTES ON GREEK AND LATIN SYNTAX. By G. BUCKLAND GREEN, M.A., Assistant-Master at the Edinburgh Academy, late Fellow of St. John's College, Oxon. Crown 8vo, 3s. 6d.

Notes and explanations on the chief difficulties of Greek and Latin Syntax, with numerous passages for exercise.

GERMAN.

A COMPANION GERMAN GRAMMAR. By H. DE B. GIBBINS, LITT.D., M.A. Crown 8vo, 1s. 6d.

SCIENCE.

THE WORLD OF SCIENCE. Including Chemistry, Heat, Light, Sound, Magnetism, Electricity, Botany, Zoology, Physiology, Astronomy, and Geology. By R. ELLIOT STEEL, M.A., F.C.S. 147 Illustrations. *Second Edition.* Crown 8vo, 2s. 6d.

ELEMENTARY LIGHT. By R. E. STEEL, M.A., F.C.S. With numerous Illustrations. Crown 8vo, 4s. 6d.

VOLUMETRIC ANALYSIS. By J. B. RUSSELL, Science Master at Burnley Grammar School. Crown 8vo, 1s.

A small Manual, containing all the necessary rules, etc., on a subject which has hitherto only been treated in expensive volumes.

ENGLISH.

THE ENGLISH CITIZEN: HIS RIGHTS AND DUTIES. By H. E. MALDEN, M.A. 1s. 6d.

A CLASS-BOOK OF DICTATION PASSAGES. By W. WILLIAMSON, M.A. Crown 8vo, 1s. 6d.

The passages are taken from recognised authors, and a few newspaper passages are included. The lists of appended words are drawn up mainly on the principle of comparison and contrast, and will form a repertoire of over 2000 difficult words.

TEST CARDS IN EUCLID AND ALGEBRA. By D. S. CALDERWOOD, Headmaster of the Normal School, Edinburgh. In three packets of 40, with Answers. 1s.

"They bear all the marks of having been prepared by a teacher of experience who knows the value of careful grading and constant repetition. Sums are specially inserted to meet all likely difficulties."—*Glasgow Herald.*

HISTORY.

ENGLISH RECORDS. A Companion to the History of England. By H. E. MALDEN, M.A. Crown 8vo, 3s. 6d.

A book which aims at concentrating information upon dates, genealogy, officials, constitutional documents, etc., which is usually found scattered in different volumes.

A SHORT HISTORY OF ROME. By J. WELLS, M.A., Fellow and Tutor of Wadham College, Oxford. With 3 Maps. *Second Edition.* Crown 8vo, 3s. 6d.

This book is intended for the Middle and Upper Forms of Public Schools and for Pass Students at the Universities. It contains copious Tables, etc.

SCHOOL EXAMINATION SERIES.

Edited by A. M. M. STEDMAN, M.A.

Crown 8vo. 2s. 6d. each.

This series is intended for the use of teachers and students, to supply ma for the former and practice for the latter. The papers are carefully grade cover the whole of the subject usually taught, and are intended to form part o ordinary class work. They may be used vivâ voce, or as a written examina This series is now in use in a large number of public and private schools, inclu Eton, Harrow, Winchester, Repton, Cheltenham, Sherborne, Haileybury, 1 chester Grammar School, Aldershot Army College, &c.

FRENCH EXAMINATION PAPERS IN MISCELLANEOUS GRAMMAR AND IDI By A. M. M. STEDMAN, M.A. *Ninth Edition.*

A KEY, issued to Tutors and Private Students only, to be had on a cation to the Publishers. *Fourth Edition.* Crown 8vo, 6s. nett.

LATIN EXAMINATION PAPERS IN MISCELLANEOUS GRAMMAR AND IDI By A. M. M. STEDMAN, M.A. *Ninth Edition.* KEY (issued as ab *Third Edition.* 6s. nett.

GREEK EXAMINATION PAPERS IN MISCELLANEOUS GRAMMAR AND IDI By A. M. M. STEDMAN, M.A. *Fifth Edition, Enlarged.* KEY (issu above). *Second Edition.* 6s. nett.

GERMAN EXAMINATION PAPERS IN MISCELLANEOUS GRAMMAR AND IDI By R. J. MORICH, Manchester Grammar School. *Fifth Edition.* (issued as above). *Second Edition.* 6s. nett.

HISTORY AND GEOGRAPHY EXAMINATION PAPERS. By C. H. SPENCE, N Clifton College. *Second Edition.*

SCIENCE EXAMINATION PAPERS. By R. E. STEEL, M.A., F.C.S. In volumes.
Part I. Chemistry.
Part II. Physics (Sound, Light, Heat, Magnetism, Electricity).

GENERAL KNOWLEDGE EXAMINATION PAPERS. By A. M. M. STEDMAN, 1 *Third Edition.* KEY (issued as above). *Second Edition.* 7s. nett.

EXAMINATION PAPERS IN BOOK-KEEPING, with Preliminary Exercises. (piled and arranged by J. T. MEDHURST, F. S. Accts. and Auditors, Lecturer at City of London College. *Third Edition.* 3s. KEY (issue above), 2s. 6d. nett.

ENGLISH LITERATURE, Questions for Examination in. Chiefly collected College Papers set at Cambridge. With an Introduction on the Stud English. By the Rev. W. W. SKEAT, D.LITT., LL.D., Professor of A1 Saxon at Cambridge University. *Third Edition, Revised.*

ARITHMETIC EXAMINATION PAPERS. By C. PENDLEBURY, M.A., S Mathematical Master, St. Paul's School. *Second Edition.* KEY (issue above), 5s.

TRIGONOMETRY EXAMINATION PAPERS. By G. H. WARD, M.A., Assi Master at St. Paul's School. *Second Edition.* KEY (issued as above), 5s.

www.ingramcontent.com/pod-product-compliance
Lightning Source LLC
Chambersburg PA
CBHW020829190426
43197CB00037B/888